low Point
mediterranean
cooking

over 60 recipes low in Points

SIMON & SCHUSTER
A VIACOM COMPANY

Becky Johnson

First published in Great Britain by Simon & Schuster UK Ltd, 2000.

A Viacom Company.

Copyright © 2000

Simon & Schuster UK Ltd.

Africa House

64–78 Kingsway

London WC2B 6AH

Photography: Steve Baxter

Styling: Marian Price

Food preparation: Sara Buenfeld

Design: Jane Humphrey

Typesetting: Stylize Digital Artwork

Printed and bound in Singapore

Weight Watchers Publications Manager: Elizabeth Egan

Weight Watchers Publications Executive: Corrina Griffin

Weight Watchers Publications Assistant: Celia Whiston

A CIP catalogue record for this book is available

from the British Library

ISBN 0 743 20913 3

Pictured on the front cover: Paella, page 43

Pictured on the back cover: Sicilian Cassata, page 60

 if vegetarian cheese and free-range eggs are used

contents

healthy
and delicious
mediterranean
meals

The shores of the warm Mediterranean sea border a large area including the South of France, Spain, Italy, Greece, Turkey, the Middle East and North Africa. The cuisines of the region are quite diverse but everyone agrees that the Mediterranean diet is an extremely healthy one. It's also ideal for Weight Watchers Members since Mediterranean cuisine is full of low Point fresh food, cooked simply and without excessive amounts of fat and sugar. Also, many of the dishes are very quick and easy to prepare so you won't need to rely on convenience food when you're pressed for time.

To use this book, try planning meals to include a variety of fresh foods. Perhaps accompany a fish, meat or vegetarian main meal with a few salads or a couple of vegetable dishes along with a good wholemeal, crusty loaf, as Points allow.

MEDITERRANEAN INGREDIENTS

Bulgar Wheat
This is steamed cracked wheat, available as coarse or fine grains. *75 g (2¾ oz) cooked serving is* **1 Point.**

Capers
These small green 'berries' are preserved by being either pickled in brine or dry-salted. *1 tablespoon of capers has* **no Points.**

Couscous
This is a durum wheat semolina from North Africa and is now available in quick-cook varieties. *100 g (3½ oz) serving of cooked couscous is* **2 Points.**

Haloumi
This cheese has a short shelf life, a distinctive elastic texture and a savoury, salty taste. It is eaten fresh and is at its best when grilled. If very salty, rinse under cold water. *2 × 20 g (¾ oz) slices are* **4 Points.**

Olive Oil
Olive oil has been used in cooking for centuries. You can make your own cooking oil spray with 1 part oil to 6 parts water in a pump action spray bottle.
1 teaspoon of olive oil is **1 Point.**
1 spray of low-fat cooking spray has **no Points.**

Orange Flower Water and Rose Water
Both these ingredients are very popular in Middle Eastern cookery where they are used in both sweet and savoury dishes. They are widely available from supermarkets in the baking section.
No Points.

Pine Kernels

This is a seed and is extracted from mature pine cones.

1 tablespoon (15 g) of pine kernels is **1½ Points.**

Porcini

Porcini are dried Italian wild mushrooms. They have a very distinctive, earthy taste and need only be used in small quantities.

6 g serving of porcini has **no Points.**

Ricotta

Ricotta is a fresh white cheese made from whey. It should be soft, creamy and sweet-tasting.

40 g (1½ oz) of ricotta is **2 Points.**

Saffron

Saffron has a distinctive aroma and a slightly bitter taste. A pinch of the threads will make a whole dish turn bright gold.

No Points.

Sun-dried Tomatoes

Only buy the dry-packed variety since they will be lower in Points. Their flavour is very intense so you only need one or two per person.

50 g (1¾ oz) portion of two sun-dried tomato halves is **1 Point.**

GROWING AND ENJOYING FRESH MEDITERRANEAN HERBS

Growing your own herbs is easy and cost-effective. It's also extremely satisfying to be able to pick them fresh from the garden or windowsill. Basil, chives, coriander, oregano, parsley, rosemary, sage and thyme can all be grown in terracotta pots in the garden or in a window box.

Keep cut herbs in polythene bags in the fridge or, if you are just about to use them, in a glass of water. Only wash them if absolutely necessary and then dry very gently.

Basil

Plant in the spring in a sun-drenched position in compost enriched soil. Since it is a delicate plant, when autumn arrives, you should bring it inside and place on a sunny windowsill. Enjoy with tomatoes, pizza and salads.

Bay Leaves

Buy a little bay leaf plant and plant it in full sun. Be careful, however, to keep it well-watered and never let it dry out. It enhances the flavour of slow-cooked stews.

Chives

Chives grow quickly in the full sun and it's good to plant them near roses since they apparently control aphids. Enjoy sprinkled over potatoes and cheesy dishes. The beautiful pink flowers are also edible so they can be used as a garnish.

Coriander

Coriander is easy to grow from seed in a sunny spot in light, rich soil. Use in salads and pasta dishes or sprinkle on soups.

Fennel

Fennel is a hardy perennial which can grow to 150 cm (5 ft) tall. Its aniseed taste complements fish and seafood very well.

Flat Leaf (French) Parsley

This vitamin rich biennial grows well in the sun or partial shade. It can be planted all year round in rich soil; replant every second season for a continuous supply. It is lovely in tabbouleh or tossed through pasta and salads.

Mint

Refreshing and soothing mint grows well in rich soil in a sunny position or in light shade. If you don't want it to take over your garden, it's best to plant it in a pot. Use generously in salads and with potatoes or use it to make mint tea.

Oregano

Oregano likes to grow in the full sun and is tolerant of dry soil. Sweet and pungent oregano is suited to most Mediterranean dishes.

Rosemary

Rosemary revels in the sun and tolerates dry soil. Trim lightly on a regular basis. Superb with lamb, potatoes and tomatoes.

Sage

Plant sage in an area with full sun and good drainage; it dislikes humidity and can be difficult in the wrong conditions. It is delicious in pasta dishes, with pork or chicken and aids the digestion of fatty foods.

Thyme

Hardy thyme thrives in stones and gravel. Its wiry leaves are full of fragrant oils which taste wonderful with meat, fish and poultry.

Mediterranean Bread: Delicious as a sweet or savoury dish.

mediterranean basics

The 'basics' of this chapter are the breads and staple sauces which define the food of the Mediterranean. All of them have the warm, aromatic and distinctive flavours, so typical of this part of the world. The Italian tomato sauce has become a real favourite in Britain in recent years as has pesto, albeit to a lesser extent. Once tried, I'm sure the others will become a regular feature on the menu at home. They are all quick and easy to prepare and full of strong, earthy flavours which are so delicious and satisfying.

MEDITERRANEAN BREAD
Focaccia

POINTS

per recipe: 17   per serving: 4

Ⓥ *Serves 4*
Preparation time: 20 minutes + 30 minutes rising
Cooking time: 10–15 minutes
Calories per serving: 240
Freezing: not recommended

This soft bread can be served with salad and cheese or as a sweet topped with fruit, yogurt and honey adding the extra Points.

---

2 teaspoons dried yeast
1 teaspoon sugar
low-fat cooking spray
2 × 145 g packets of instant pizza mix
1 teaspoon oil, for greasing
2 or 3 sprigs of fresh rosemary
sea salt

1 In a small mixing bowl, combine 225 ml (8 fl oz) warm water, the yeast and sugar and leave for 15 minutes until frothy. Spray a 28 × 18 cm (11 × 7-inch) shallow baking tin with low-fat cooking spray.
2 Put the pizza mix into a large bowl and make a well in the centre. Add the frothed yeast and mix to a soft dough. Turn out on to a floured surface and knead for 2 or 3 minutes until smooth in texture.

3 Press into the prepared baking tin, pushing the dough into the corners. Cover with clingfilm, oiled with 1 teaspoon, and leave to rise in a warm place for about 30 minutes or until doubled in height.
4 Meanwhile, preheat the oven to Gas Mark 7/220°C/425°F. Make dimples all over the surface of the risen dough with your fingers and sprinkle with the rosemary and sea salt.
5 Bake for 10–15 minutes until golden.

VARIATION To make a sweet version, add 1 tablespoon of sugar to the dry pizza mix before adding the yeast. Sprinkle a little demerara sugar over the finished dough in the tray instead of the rosemary and salt. The Points per serving will be 4½.

GARLIC YOGURT SAUCE
Sarimsakli

POINTS

per recipe: 4½   per serving: 1

Ⓥ *Serves 4*
Preparation time: 2 minutes
Calories per serving: 25
Freezing: not recommended

This tangy Turkish sauce is great when you're in a rush since it's so quick and easy.

---

200 ml (7 fl oz) thick and creamy low-fat plain yogurt
1 garlic clove, crushed with a little salt
a small bunch of mint or dill, chopped finely
a pinch of paprika, to garnish

1 Beat the yogurt and garlic together in a bowl. Mix in the mint and refrigerate.
2 Serve chilled, garnished with a little paprika.

COOK'S TIP This can be used as a dip or as an accompaniment to lamb or grilled vegetables adding extra Points.

BASIC PIZZA DOUGH

POINTS

per recipe: 19   per serving: 4½

Ⓥ *Serves 4*

Preparation time: ½ hour + 35 minutes rising

Cooking time: 10–15 minutes

Calories per serving: 325

Freezing: not recommended

---

7 g sachet of dried yeast

a pinch of sugar

350 g (12 oz) strong plain white bread flour, plus extra for dusting

2 teaspoons olive oil

½ teaspoon salt

---

1 Mix the yeast with the sugar and 150 ml (¼ pint) warm water and leave for 10 minutes until frothy. Sift the flour into a large bowl and make a well in the centre. Pour in the yeast mixture, oil and salt. Mix together with a palette knife first and then use your hands until the dough comes together.

2 Tip out on to a floured surface and knead vigourously for 10 minutes. Place in a clean oiled bowl, cover with a damp tea towel or piece of clingfilm and leave to rise in a warm place for 30 minutes until doubled in size.

3 Preheat the oven to Gas Mark 9/ 240°C/475°F. Punch the dough and push it down. Then leave it to rise again for 5 minutes: Roll out the dough or stretch it with your fingers, to a 30 cm (12 inch) circle on a large floured baking sheet or, for mini pizzas, divide into 4 and stretch each to a circle measuring 10 cm (4 inches).

4 Add the toppings of your choice and bake for 10–15 minutes until golden and crisp around the edges.

COOK'S TIPS When kneading the dough it should change in texture from loose and floury to smooth, soft and elastic. If it doesn't, then you haven't kneaded long enough or hard enough!

For a really authentic pizza base, try using the 'oo' flour, which is the Italian extra fine flour.

MARGHERITA PIZZA

POINTS

per recipe: 26   per serving: 6½

Ⓥ *Serves 4*

Preparation time: 5 minutes

Cooking time: 10–15 minutes

Calories per serving: 305

Freezing: not recommended

---

1 quantity basic pizza dough (see above)

8 tablespoons passata (sieved tomatoes) or any jar of tomato pasta sauce or Italian tomato sauce (see below)

---

115 g (4 oz) half-fat mozzarella cheese, sliced thinly

2 garlic cloves, peeled and chopped finely

a pinch of dried oregano

fresh basil leaves

1 tablespoon extra virgin olive oil

salt and freshly ground black pepper

---

1 Preheat the oven to Gas Mark 9/ 240°C/475°F. Spread the dough with the tomato sauce, avoiding the edges.

2 Scatter over the cheese, garlic, herbs and salt and pepper. Drizzle with the olive oil and bake for 10–15 minutes or until the edges are crisp and golden.

VARIATIONS A wide variety of different herbs can be used to great effect in this recipe: try rosemary, thyme or coriander or sprinkle with roughly chopped watercress.

Use a ready-made 30 cm (12-inch) pizza base. The Points per serving will be 6½.

ITALIAN TOMATO SAUCE

POINTS

per recipe: ½   per serving: 0

Ⓥ *Serves 4 (as a pasta sauce)*

Preparation time: 10 minutes

Cooking time: 30 minutes

Calories per serving: 35

Freezing: not recommended

An excellent accompaniment to fish, poultry or meat; add the Points as necessary.

---

low-fat cooking spray

2 onions, chopped finely

2 large garlic cloves, chopped finely

300 g (10½ oz) canned chopped tomatoes

1 teaspoon honey

a large handful of basil or parsley

salt and freshly ground black pepper

---

1 Spray a large saucepan with the cooking spray and put over a medium heat. Gently fry the onions and garlic until softened, about 10 minutes, and then add the canned tomatoes, salt, pepper and honey.

2 Cook for 20 minutes and then stir in the basil or parsley and serve.

PESTO

POINTS

per recipe: 7½   per serving: 2

(V) *Serves 4 (as a pasta sauce)*
*Preparation time: 2 minutes with a
food processor, 10 minutes with a
pestle and mortar*
Calories per serving: 85
Freezing: not recommended

Full of intense and wonderfully
aromatic flavours.

1½ tablespoons pine kernels
1 large garlic clove, chopped
1 tablespoon olive oil
50 g (1¾ oz) fresh basil
25 g (1 oz) freshly grated parmesan cheese
sea salt and freshly ground black pepper

1 Toast the pine kernels in a non-
stick frying pan until lighly coloured.
Put in a food processor with the garlic,
oil and a little salt. Process to a coarse
purée. Add a little water if the mixture
is too dry to purée effectively.
2 Add the basil and cheese and
process to a paste. Then, with the
motor running, gradually pour in
2 tablespoons of water. Taste and
season, then serve.

COOK'S TIP Once made, the pesto
will keep in the fridge for up to 4 days.

WEIGHT WATCHERS TIPS Pesto
is quite high in Points but its strong
flavour means you only need to use
a little as a sauce for pasta.
    You can also brush fish or chicken
with small amounts and then grill.
It's great on toast or with baked
potatoes too, adding the extra Points.

VARIATIONS Try using mint or
coriander instead of basil.

GREEK GARLIC SAUCE
Skorthalia

POINTS

per recipe: 10   per serving: 2½

(V) *Serves 4*
*Preparation time: 5 minutes +
10 minutes soaking*
Calories per serving: 115
Freezing: not recommended

Serve this sauce with steamed
vegetables and grilled meats or fish.

2 or 3 garlic cloves, chopped
75 g (2¾ oz) fresh wholemeal breadcrumbs
juice of 1 lemon
1 tablespoon olive oil
50 g (1¾ oz) ground almonds
salt

1 Blend the garlic, breadcrumbs and
lemon juice in a liquidiser with a
little salt until smooth.
2 With the motor still running, pour
in the oil and 3 tablespoons of water.
Add the almonds and blend briefly
to make a runny sauce. Add a little
more water if necessary to thin the
sauce. Serve or chill until needed.

WEIGHT WATCHERS TIP The
Points per serving are per serving of
the sauce only.

**Greek Garlic
Sauce: In Greek
homes, this
garlic sauce is
indispensible.**

appetisers
and light meals

In the Mediterranean, appetisers are often served together and eaten as a whole meal. They are called tapas in Spain, mezze in Greece, antipasta in Italy. They reflect the relaxed way of life of the Mediterranean and are meant to be enjoyed slowly, perhaps with a glass of wine or beer. They can also be served as starters, finger food for drinks parties, buffets or as part of a light lunch or supper.

STUFFED 'VINE' LEAVES
Dolmades

POINTS	
per recipe: 13½	per serving: 3½

Ⓥ   *Serves 4*
Preparation time: 1 hour
Cooking time: 1 hour
Calories per serving: 260
Freezing: recommended

Authentic Greek 'dolmades' are wrapped in vine or fig leaves but this recipe has been adapted to use the more readily available Savoy cabbage leaves. Cabbage leaves also allow for more filling! Serve hot or cold with lemon slices and fresh dill sprigs or mint, or with Tzatziki (page 13).

2 tablespoons pine kernels

16 leaves of Savoy cabbage

125 g (4½ oz) long grain rice, uncooked

1 onion, chopped finely

8 dried apricots, chopped finely

4 tablespoons chopped fresh parsley

4 tablespoons chopped fresh dill

4 tablespoons chopped fresh mint

zest and juice of 1 lemon

1 tablespoon olive oil

sea salt and freshly ground black pepper

1 Put the pine kernels in a dry frying pan and toast over a low heat until they are beginning to brown. Keep an eye on them to make sure that they don't burn.

2 Wash the the cabbage leaves, then blanch them in batches of 5 or 6 in boiling, salted water for 5 seconds. Take them out with tongs and drain.

3 Mix all the remaining ingredients together in a bowl.

4 Line the base of a large saucepan with a couple of cabbage leaves. To fill the other leaves, place 1 or 2 tablespoons of the stuffing at the stalk end of the leaf and roll once. Then fold in the sides and continue to roll. Secure with cocktail sticks and put in the saucepan. When one layer is complete, sprinkle over some seasoning and then start another.

5 When all the leaves are used up, place a small inverted plate inside the saucepan and over the top of the stuffed leaves to weigh them all down. Carefully add 425 ml (¾ pint) boiling water to the pan. Cover and simmer for 50 minutes.

Stuffed 'Vine' Leaves: This Greek starter is full of interesting flavours.

**Aubergine Sauce:
Delicious with
toasted pitta.**

HUMMOUS

POINTS	
per recipe: $7\frac{1}{2}$	per serving: $1\frac{1}{2}$

v *Serves 6*
Preparation time: 5 minutes
Calories per serving: 75
Freezing: not recommended

This Mediterranean chick-pea dip is one of my all time favourite foods. It can be eaten on its own with pitta bread and salad or as a dip. It can also be stirred into any number of dishes to add texture and flavour. This quick and easy recipe uses canned chick-peas.

1 tablespoon light tahini paste
400 g can of chick-peas, drained and rinsed
1 teaspoon sesame oil
1 garlic clove, chopped
juice of 1 or 2 lemons
2 teaspoons ground cumin (optional)
sea salt and freshly ground pepper

1 Stir the tahini paste in the jar, as it separates easily, then divide all the ingredients into two batches.
2 Put one batch into the food processor with 150 ml (¼ pint) of water. Taste and then adjust the seasoning.
3 Repeat with the other batch, mix the two batches together and serve.

COOK'S TIP Hummous will keep in the fridge for up to 4 days.

AUBERGINE SAUCE
Baba Ghanoush

POINTS	
per recipe: 0	per serving: 0

v *Serves 4*
Preparation time: 10 minutes
Cooking time: 1 hour
Calories per serving: 45
Freezing: not recommended

This Mediterranean sauce has a slightly smoky flavour. It is delicious with pasta or grilled vegetables. You can also enjoy it as a dip.

1 kg (2 lb 4 oz) aubergines
½ small onion, chopped coarsely
1 or 2 garlic cloves
juice of 1 lemon
2 tablespoons chopped flat leaf parsley
4 black olives, sliced (optional)
salt and freshly ground black pepper

1 Preheat the oven to Gas Mark 6/ 200°C/400°F. Prick the aubergines with a fork and lay them on a baking tray. Roast for 1 hour or until charred and soft, then leave to cool.
2 Slit the cooled aubergines open. Spoon the flesh out of the aubergines and into a sieve. Squeeze out the juices.
3 Process the aubergine flesh in a food processor with the onion, garlic and lemon juice.
4 Taste and adjust the seasoning, then serve sprinkled with the parsley and olives if using.

YOGURT AND CUCUMBER DIP
Tzatziki

POINTS	
per recipe: 5	per serving: 1

v *Serves 4*
Preparation time: 10 minutes + chilling time
Calories per serving: 35
Freezing: recommended

This sauce is found all over the Eastern Mediterranean and can be served as a dip or as an accompaniment to grilled fish and meats. It's also delicious as a salad dressing.

1 teaspoon white wine vinegar
225 ml (8 fl oz) thick and creamy low-fat plain yogurt
1 small cucumber, peeled and chopped finely or grated
1 tablespoon finely chopped fresh mint, plus extra leaves to garnish
salt and freshly ground black pepper

1 Mix together the vinegar, yogurt and seasoning in a bowl.
2 Sandwich the cucumber between two tea towels or two pieces of kitchen paper and squeeze out any excess water. Then mix it with the yogurt sauce and the chopped mint.
3 Check the seasoning then refrigerate and serve lightly chilled garnished with the mint leaves.

MINI PIZZAS

Makes 4 mini pizzas
Preparation time: 10 minutes or 1
hour + 10 minutes if you make your
own bases
Cooking time: 10 minutes
Calories per serving: 245 (tomato and
onion); 340 (pepper and courgette);
335 (tuna, sweetcorn and capers)
Freezing: not recommended

All these recipes make 4 mini
pizzas and they are delicious with
ready-made or home-made dough
(page 8).

**Grilled Peppers
and Courgette
Mini Pizza: The
ideal snack.**

Roasted Tomato and Onion Mini Pizzas Ⓥ

POINTS	
per recipe: 16	per serving: 4

low-fat cooking spray
2 red onions, chopped into thin wedges
2 garlic cloves, sliced
4 sprigs of thyme or rosemary
4 × 10 cm (4-inch) pizza bases
4 tablespoons passata (sieved tomatoes)
or home-made Italian tomato sauce
(page 8)
4 sun-dried tomatoes, chopped finely

Zesty Grilled Peppers and Courgette Mini Pizzas Ⓥ

POINTS	
per recipe: 20	per serving: 5

low-fat cooking spray
2 red peppers, cut into thin wedges
2 courgettes, sliced
4 × 10 cm (4-inch) pizza bases
225 g (8 oz) low-fat soft cheese
1 garlic clove, crushed
zest and juice of 1 lemon
sea salt and freshly ground black pepper

Tuna, Sweetcorn and Caper Mini Pizzas

POINTS	
per recipe: 20½	per serving: 5

4 × 10 cm (4-inch) pizza bases
4 tablespoons passata (sieved
tomatoes) or home-made Italian
tomato sauce (page 8)
200 g can of sweetcorn, drained
200 g can of tuna in brine, drained
juice of 1 lemon
1 tablespoon olive oil

1 Preheat the oven to Gas Mark 9/
240°C/475°F. Spray a baking sheet
with the cooking spray. In a small
bowl, toss the onion wedges together
with the garlic and herbs and put in
the oven to roast for 10–15 minutes.
Meanwhile, spread the pizza bases
with the tomato sauce.
2 Place the roasted vegetables on
top of the pizzas and scatter over the
sun-dried tomatoes, if using. Bake for
10–15 minutes or until the bases are
crisp and golden. Serve hot or cold.

1 Preheat the oven to Gas Mark 9/
240°C/475°F and preheat the grill to
high. Spray a baking tray with the
cooking spray and put the vegetables
on it. Place the vegetables under the
grill for 5 minutes or until they have
started to blacken. Meanwhile, spread
the pizza bases with the low-fat soft
cheese.
2 Put the hot grilled vegetables in a
bowl and toss with the garlic, lemon
juice and zest. Season. Pile on to
the pizzas and bake in the oven for
10–15 minutes or until the bases are
crisp and golden.

2 tablespoons capers, rinsed and drained
salt and freshly ground black pepper

1 Preheat the oven to Gas Mark 9/
240°C/475°F. Spread the top of each
pizza base with a tablespoon of
the passata or tomato sauce.
2 In a bowl, mix together the
sweetcorn and tuna with the lemon
juice and olive oil, then pile on top
of the pizzas. Finish with the capers
and seasoning.
3 Bake for 10–15 minutes or until
the pizza crusts are crisp and golden.

FALAFELS

POINTS

per recipe: 8	per serving: ½

V Makes 20

*Preparation time: overnight soaking +
20 minutes + 50 minutes standing time
Cooking time: 25 minutes
Calories per serving: 55
Freezing: recommended*

These delicious and satisfying
Mediterranean patties are very low
in fat. Enjoy falafels in warmed pitta
breads with salad or Lebanese Bulgar
Wheat and Herb Salad (page 26) and
Garlic Yogurt Sauce (page 7), adding
the extra Points.

75 g (2¾ oz) bulgar wheat
700 ml (1¼ pints) boiling water
*225 g (8 oz) dried chick-peas, soaked
in water overnight in the refrigerator*
1 garlic clove
4 spring onions, chopped finely
3 tablespoons flat leaf parsley, chopped
1 teaspoon ground coriander
1 teaspoon ground cumin
¼ teaspoon cayenne pepper
1 tablespoon lemon juice
½ teaspoon bicarbonate of soda
low-fat cooking spray
salt and freshly ground black pepper

1 Rinse the bulgar wheat in a sieve.
Place in a bowl, cover with the
boiling water and leave to swell
for 20 minutes.

2 Drain the chick-peas and place in a
food processor with the bulgar wheat
and all the other ingredients, except
the cooking spray. Process to a paste-
like consistency. Cover and leave to
stand for 30 minutes.

3 With moistened hands, shape
tablespoons of the mixture into 20
thin patties, about 4 cm (1½ inches)
in diameter.

4 Spray a large frying pan with the
cooking spray and then fry the patties
in batches for 3 minutes on each
side. To check that they are cooked
through, break one in half: the colour
should be even all the way through to
the middle. If not, increase the
cooking time by a minute.

MUSHROOM PÂTÉ ON TOASTED FRENCH BREAD
Mushroom Crostini

POINTS

per recipe: 7	per serving: 1½

V Serves 4

*Preparation time: 15 minutes +
20 minutes soaking
Cooking time: 25 minutes
Calories per serving: 130
Freezing: not recommended*

Known as crostini in Italy, these
toasts are a famous part of Tuscan
antipasta.

25 g (1 oz) porcini mushrooms
1 tablespoon olive oil
2 shallots, chopped finely
2 garlic cloves, crushed
*½ teaspon dried oregano or
1 tablespoon fresh oregano*
juice of ½ lemon

150 g (5½ oz) button mushrooms
*1 white baguette (about 125 g/4½ oz),
cut into thin diagonal slices*
sea salt and freshly ground black pepper
*a handful of fresh parsley, oregano or
chives, to garnish*

1 Soak the dried mushrooms in
150 ml (¼ pint) of warm water
for 20 minutes.

2 Heat the olive oil in a frying pan,
then gently fry the shallots and garlic
until softened and golden, about
5 minutes.

3 Add the soaked dried mushrooms
and their soaking liquid, the oregano
and lemon juice to the pan. Cover
and simmer for 15 minutes.

4 Meanwhile, coarsely chop the
button mushrooms. Add them
to the pan and turn up the heat.
Cook quickly, without a lid, for
5 minutes or until most of the liquid
has evaporated. Taste and season.
Leave to cool.

5 Preheat the grill to high. Put the
cooled mixture in a food processor
and pulse to make a coarse pâté.

6 Toast the slices of bread under
the grill and then generously spread
each one with the mushroom
mixture. Garnish with the parsley
or oregano or chives.

COOK'S TIP Porcini are now
readily available in supermarkets and
delicatessans. See the ingredients list
at the start of the book for more
information.

VARIATIONS Replace the baguette
with different varieties of bread
such as wholemeal, soda or ciabatta
adjusting the Points accordingly.

Italian Garlic Toast: A tasty alternative to garlic bread.

ITALIAN GARLIC TOASTS
Bruschetta

POINTS

per recipe: 9½   per serving: 2½

Ⓥ *Serves 4*
Preparation time: 2 minutes
Cooking time: 2 minutes
Calories per serving: 140
Freezing: not recommended

This very simple recipe can be used as a base for savoury toppings like cheese and tomato or ham and mustard.

4 thick slices of bread, from a bloomer or rustic loaf
1 garlic clove
4 teaspoons extra virgin olive oil
basil leaves, to garnish
sea salt

1 Toast the bread until golden on both sides under a preheated grill. Cut the garlic clove in half and rub the cut side over the toast.
2 Dribble over the olive oil and scatter over the sea salt. Serve while still hot, garnished with the basil leaves.

HERBY BEAN PÂTÉ
Bessara

POINTS

per recipe: 7   per serving: 1½

Ⓥ *Serves 4*
Preparation time: 2 minutes
Calories per serving: 115
Freezing: not recommended

This Egyptian recipe tastes as fresh as it looks.

225 g can of broad beans, drained, rinsed and skinned
a small bunch of parsley, chopped
a small bunch of coriander, chopped
1 fresh chilli, de-seeded and chopped finely
2 garlic cloves, chopped finely
1½ teaspoons ground cumin
2 tablespoons olive oil
salt
juice and zest of 1 lemon
1 small red onion, sliced thinly

1 Put all the ingredients except the lemon zest and red onion in a food processor with 2 tablespoons of water. Process until smooth. If the pâté is too dry, add more water.
2 Refrigerate and serve chilled. Garnish with lemon zest and onion slices.

VARIATION This is also delicious with sun-dried tomatoes. Stir in 4 finely chopped halves of sun-dried tomatoes which have been soaked for ½ hour in 2 tablespoons of hot water, adding 1 Point per serving.

GAZPACHO

POINTS

per recipe: 6½   per serving: 1

Ⓥ *Serves 6*
Preparation time: 25 minutes + 10 minutes soaking + 2–3 hours chilling
Calories per serving: 115
Freezing: not recommended

2 medium slices of stale bread, crusts removed

1 kg (2 lb 4 oz) ripe tomatoes, peeled and chopped
½ cucumber, chopped coarsley
1 small red onion, chopped roughly
2 garlic cloves, crushed
1 green or red pepper, de-seeded and chopped
2 tablespoons olive oil
2 tablespoons wine vinegar
2 tablespoons chopped fresh parsley
a handful of fresh basil or mint plus a few leaves for garnish
sea salt and freshly ground black pepper
ice cubes, to garnish

1 Soak the bread in water for 10 minutes, squeeze it a little and then blend in a food processor with the remaining ingredients. Taste and season.
2 Empty into a bowl, cover and chill for 2–3 hours.
3 Serve chilled, garnished with basil and ice cubes.

VARIATION This soup does not have to be blended. For a chunkier version, just finely chop all the vegetables and mix with the other ingredients.

Gazpacho: This Spanish soup is fantastic on a hot day.

**Soupe au Pistou:
The delicious
French version of
Italian minestrone.**

SOUPE AU PISTOU

Ⓥ *Serves 4*

Preparation time: 25 minutes +
soaking overnight
Cooking time: 50 minutes
Calories per serving: 320
Freezing: not recommended

This soup is full of delicious and
nutritious vegetables, beans and pasta
and the addition of pistou, which
is like pesto but without the pine
kernels, gives it a wonderfully
aromatic flavour.

low-fat cooking spray
1 onion, chopped
2 leeks, chopped finely
400 g can of chopped tomatoes
2 small potatoes, diced finely
350 g (12 oz) courgettes, diced finely
2 carrots, diced finely
300 g can of haricot beans, drained
100 g (3¹/₂ oz) green beans, cut into
quarters
a bunch of flat leaf parsley, chopped
50 g (1³/₄ oz) spaghettini, broken into
short pieces
salt and freshly ground black pepper

FOR THE PISTOU

1 bunch of basil
1 large garlic clove, crushed
2 tablespoons olive oil
25 g (1 oz) freshly grated parmesan
cheese
1 tablespoon low-fat soft cheese

1 Spray a large saucepan with the
cooking spray and then sauté the
onion and leeks, adding a little
water if they stick. After 2 minutes,
add the other vegetables and the
beans. Mix everything together and
then pour over 2 litres (3¹/₂ pints)
hot water. Cover and simmer for
30 minutes.

2 While the soup is simmering,
make the pistou by processing
the basil, garlic and oil in a food
processor until smooth. If it is too
dry, add a little water. Scrape down
the jug and then add the cheeses.
Pulse quickly until mixed in.

3 Season, add the pasta and parsley
to the soup and cook for a further
10 minutes. Just before serving, stir
in the pistou, saving a little to blob
on top.

BORLOTTI BEAN AND ROSEMARY SOUP

Ⓥ *if using vegetable stock*

Serves 6

Preparation time: 20 minutes +
soaking overnight
Cooking time: 1¹/₄ hours
Calories per serving: 135
Freezing: not recommended

This thick and comforting Italian
soup makes a satisfying lunch.

low-fat cooking spray
2 garlic cloves, crushed
1 large onion, diced
1 large carrot, diced
250 g (9 oz) borlotti beans, soaked
overnight in water
8 sprigs of rosemary, chopped finely
2 litres (3¹/₂ pints) chicken or
vegetable stock
salt and freshly ground black pepper

1 Spray a large saucepan with the
low-fat cooking spray, then gently
fry the garlic, onion and carrot until
beginning to soften, about 4 minutes.
Add a tablespoon of water if they stick.

2 Drain the beans and then add
the beans, rosemary and stock to
the saucepan. Bring to the boil.
Boil for 10 minutes, skimming the
top occasionally and then keep at a
low simmer for 40–50 minutes or
until the beans are tender.

3 Take out half the soup and
liquidise it carefully since it will
be hot. Then put it back into the
pot and stir. Taste to check the
seasoning and then serve.

COOK'S TIP You can use canned
beans to reduce the cooking time.
Add 3 × 300 g cans of drained and
rinsed beans to the sautéed vegetables.
Reduce the stock to 1.2 litres (2 pints)
and the cooking time to 10 minutes.

VARIATIONS You could also use
black beans, pintos, or haricot beans
instead of borlotti beans.

Add 50 g (1³/₄ oz) small pasta to
make it even more hearty but do
not liquidise the soup. The Points
per serving will be 1.

FRENCH SANDWICH
Pan Bagnat

POINTS

per recipe: 14   per serving: 2½

Serves 6
Preparation time: 10 minutes +
2 hours infusing time
Calories per serving: 205
Freezing: not recommended

This was created in France for labourers to take out to the fields for lunch.

6 medium crusty rolls
2 tablespoons white wine vinegar or lemon juice
2 garlic cloves, crushed
4 tomatoes, sliced thinly
1 onion
2 red pepper, de-seeded and cut into thin strips
2 × 200 g cans of tuna in brine
a large handful of basil, torn coarsely
sea salt and freshly ground pepper

1 Slice the rolls in half horizontally. Drizzle the vinegar or lemon juice over the cut faces of the bread. Scatter the garlic and seasoning on top.

2 Arrange the vegetables, tuna, basil and olives, if using, on one half of each roll and then place the other half on top. Wrap the rolls in foil or a clean tea towel. Place a weight, such as a breadboard, on top and leave for at least 2 hours before serving.

VARIATIONS Vegetarians could replace the tuna with 200 g (7 oz) vegetarian low-fat cheese. The Points per serving would be 3½.

You could also add 12 black olives in step 2. The Points will remain the same.

FILO PARCELS

POINTS

per recipe: 14   per serving: ½

V *Makes about 30*
Preparation time: 35 minutes
Cooking time: 15 minutes
Calories per serving: 45
Freezing: not recommended

These little Greek pies can be stuffed with any assortment of tasty fillings. Here is a very typical mixture of grated carrot, pine kernels, currants and herbs.

50 g (1¾ oz) pine kernels
1 tablespoon cumin seeds
175 g (6 oz) carrots, grated coarsely
2 tablespoons currants, soaked in 2 tablespoons of water for 10 minutes
1 tablespoon ground cinnamon
2 tablespoons chopped fresh parsley or coriander

low-fat cooking spray
1 onion, chopped finely
2 garlic cloves, chopped finely
10 sheets of fresh or frozen filo pastry, defrosted if frozen
salt and freshly ground black pepper

1 Toast the pine kernels and cumin seeds in a dry frying pan until golden brown. Then mix them together in a bowl with the carrots, currants, cinnamon, herbs and seasoning.

2 Spray the frying pan with the cooking spray and fry the onion and garlic for 4 minutes. Add 2 tablespoons of water if they stick. Add the fried onion to the other ingredients and mix well.

3 Preheat the oven to Gas Mark 4/ 180°C/350°F and spray two baking sheets with cooking spray.

4 Cut the filo pastry into three parts lengthways. Keep them covered with a damp tea towel until you are ready to use them.

5 For the next step, leave the sheets of filo pastry on the stack while spraying them with cooking spray and adding the filling. If you peel them off to work on them, they will crumble and stick to the counter. Working with three strips of pastry at a time, spray with the cooking spray and place a heaped tablespoon of the filling on to the top right hand corner of each strip. Fold down the corner to make a triangle and continue to flip the filled triangle down the length of the filo strip to wrap in the pastry. Place the filo triangles on a baking sheet and spray with a little more cooking spray. Repeat to use up all the filling.

6 Bake the parcels for 15 minutes until crisp and a deep golden brown colour.

French Sandwich: Perfect for picnics and outdoor lunches.

Salade Niçoise:
An authentic
version of the
famous salad
from Nice in
the South of
France.

salads

Salads and cold vegetable dishes are present at almost every Mediterranean meal and perhaps they are the reason people in the Mediterranean seem to live longer... All of the salads in this chapter can be meals in themselves or they can be a side dish. Dress the salads and vegetables at the last possible minute, unless they are marinating, and always try to use the best quality ingredients.

SALADE NIÇOISE

POINTS	
per recipe: 13½	per serving: 3½

Serves 4
Preparation time: 20 minutes
Cooking time: 15 minutes
Calories per serving: 290
Freezing: not recommended

1 teaspoon salt

a sprig of mint

450 g (1 lb) new potatoes, scrubbed

4 eggs

200 g (7 oz) green beans, tailed

200 g can of tuna in brine, drained

225 g (8 oz) cherry tomatoes, halved

1 small red onion, sliced thinly

12 black olives

a bunch of basil, chopped roughly

2 Little Gem lettuce, separated into leaves and washed

FOR THE VINAIGRETTE

juice and zest of 1 lemon

1 teaspoon whole-grain mustard

2 tablespoons virtually fat-free fromage frais

salt and freshly ground black pepper

1 Bring two pans of water to the boil. To one, add the teaspoon of salt and a sprig of mint. Cook the new potatoes for 10–15 minutes or until just tender. In the other pan, boil the eggs for 10 minutes. Steam the green beans over one of the pans until just cooked, about 2–4 minutes.

2 Drain the eggs and immediately put them under a cold tap to cool them rapidly. Then slice them into quarters and put them in a large bowl with all the other ingredients for the salad. When the potatoes are cooked, drain and add them to the bowl.

3 Whisk together all the vinaigrette ingredients and then pour the vinaigrette over the salad. Toss everything together very gently. Check the seasoning and serve.

COOK'S TIP Putting the eggs into boiling water and then cooling them rapidly under the cold tap ensures that the yolks stay a lovely yellow colour.

VARIATIONS Other ingredients to try are capers, red peppers, fresh tuna, anchovies and flat leaf parsley, adding the Points as necessary.

ROASTED PEPPER SALAD

POINTS

per recipe: 1½   per serving: ½

 Serves 4

Preparation time: 15 minutes

Cooking time: 10 minutes

Calories per serving: 95

Freezing: not recommended

This simple Italian recipe is ideal on a hot day with bread and Hummous (page 13).

6 red peppers, or a mixture of red, yellow and orange peppers

1 tablespoon balsamic vinegar

2 teaspoons extra virgin olive oil

1 garlic clove, crushed

salt and freshly ground black pepper

a bunch of fresh basil, to garnish

1 Preheat the grill to high. Put the peppers on a grill tray, whole if they will fit, or halved if not, but skin side up.

2 Grill for 5 minutes on all sides so that the peppers are charred and blackened all over. Leave to cool for a few minutes and then place in a plastic bag. Seal the bag and leave to cool.

3 Meanwhile put the vinegar, oil, garlic and seasoning in a screw top jar, put on the lid and shake, or whisk them together in a small bowl.

4 When the peppers are cool enough to handle, remove them from the plastic bag, peel off the skins and remove all the seeds and tops. Slice them into quarters. Put into a serving dish and pour over the vinaigrette. Garnish with the basil leaves and serve.

COOK'S TIP Putting the peppers in a plastic bag steams them further and enables the skin to be easily peeled off.

WARM GOATS' CHEESE SALAD

POINTS

per recipe: 17½   per serving: 4½

 Serves 4

Preparation and cooking time: 15 minutes

Calories per serving: 180

Freezing: not recommended

Although France is perhaps best known for its good quality goats' cheeses, there are some excellent ones from Wales and the West Country too. The flavours vary from very ripe and strong to mild and fresh, so you can experiment a bit with them.

175 g (6 oz) mixed salad leaves (such as rocket, frisée, oak-leaf, lamb's lettuce, radicchio), washed

a bunch of mixed summer herbs, such as basil, chervil, coriander or parsley, washed

200 g (7 oz) baguette

100 g (3½ oz) goats' cheese with a crumbly/soft texture, such as a crottin

FOR THE VINAIGRETTE

1 tablespoon balsamic vinegar

2 teaspoons whole-grain mustard

2 tablespoons virtually fat-free fromage frais

salt and freshly ground black pepper

1 Put the salad leaves in a serving bowl with the herbs.

2 Heat the grill to high. Cut the bread into 20 diagonal slices to make large croûtons and spread each with a little goats' cheese. Pop the croûtons under the grill for a few minutes or until beginning to brown at the edges.

3 Meanwhile put all the vinaigrette ingredients into a screw top jar, put on the lid and shake. Pour over the salad and toss together.

4 Place the croûtons on top of the salad and serve immediately.

WEIGHT WATCHERS TIP

I have not found a low-fat goats' cheese but the fat content does vary from cheese to cheese so do check before you buy. Because the flavour is so pronounced, however, you only need to use a little to get a great taste.

VARIATION Try using 2 teaspoons of walnut or hazelnut oil instead of 2 tablespoons of fromage frais. These oils have a delicious nutty flavour which is excellent in this salad. The Points per serving will be 5.

Roasted Pepper Salad: Roasting brings out the delicious sweetness of the peppers.

LEBANESE BULGAR WHEAT AND HERB SALAD
Tabbouleh

Ⓥ Serves 4

Preparation time: 30 minutes soaking time + 10 minutes + 10–30 minutes marinating

Calories per serving: 145

Freezing: not recommended

125 g (4½ oz) bulgar wheat

425 ml (¾ pint) boiling water

a large bunch of parsley, trimmed

a bunch of mint, washed

½ cucumber, diced finely

1 small red onion, diced finely

1 large tomato, diced finely

FOR THE VINAIGRETTE

juice of 2 lemons

3 tablespoons tomato juice

a pinch of sugar

salt and freshly ground black pepper

1 Rinse the bulgar wheat in a sieve and then put it in a large bowl. Pour over the boiling water and leave to swell for 20 minutes.

2 Meanwhile, chop the parsley and mint and mix with the vegetables in a serving dish.

3 Mix the lemon juice, tomato juice, sugar and seasoning together in a bowl with a whisk.

4 Drain the bulgar wheat of any excess water. Mix in with the vegetables and herbs and pour over the dressing.

5 Toss together and leave to marinate for at least 10 minutes and ideally 30 minutes before serving. Just before serving, taste and adjust the seasoning and add more lemon juice if necessary.

Lebanese Bulgar Wheat and Herb Salad: This Lebanese salad is wonderfully satisfying.

ITALIAN BREAD SALAD
Panzanella

Ⓥ Serves 4

Preparation time: 10 minutes + 30 minutes marinating

Calories per serving: 155

Freezing: not recommended

4 thick slices of bread

6 ripe tomatoes, diced

½ cucumber, diced

1 red onion, diced

a small bunch of parsley, chopped

2 sprigs of rosemary, chopped very finely

2 teaspoons tomato purée mixed with 4 tablespoons of water

2 tablespoons red wine vinegar

salt and freshly ground black pepper

This salad is substantial enough to enjoy as a meal. It needs to be made with a good, coarse country bread. It's best left for 30 minutes before serving so that the bread can soak up all the flavours.

1 Tear the bread into small pieces and put in a large serving bowl. Sprinkle a little water over it to just moisten it but not make it wet.

2 Add all the other ingredients and toss together.

3 Leave for 30 minutes and then serve.

CARROT AND ORANGE SALAD

 Serves 4

Preparation time: 5 minutes
Calories per serving: 85
Freezing: not recommended

This Moroccan salad is traditionally served before the meal as an appetiser but then left on the table to accompany the rest of the meal.

3 oranges

2 carrots, peeled and grated coarsely

a small bunch of coriander, chopped

1 tablespoon orange flower water

a pinch of ground cinnamon

FOR THE DRESSING

3 tablespoons orange juice

1 tablespoon lemon juice

1 teaspoon honey

salt and freshly ground black pepper

1 Peel the oranges and segment them. Mix them together with the carrots and coriander, reserving some coriander for the garnish in a bowl.

2 Whisk together all the ingredients for the dressing until the honey has dissolved.

3 Pour the dressing over the salad, toss everything together and place in a serving bowl.

4 Sprinkle over the orange flower water, cinnamon and fresh coriander, then serve.

VARIATIONS Replace the oranges with 3 apples. The Points will remain the same.

Sprinkle over 2 teaspoons of toasted sesame seeds in step 5.

Greek Salad:
A delicious
traditional salad
from Greece.

GREEK SALAD

POINTS

| per recipe: $16\frac{1}{2}$ | per serving: 4 |

V Serves 4

Preparation time: 10 minutes
Calories per serving: 225
Freezing: not recommended

200 g (7 oz) feta cheese, diced

1 small cucumber, quartered and sliced into wedges

8 ripe tomatoes, cut into wedges

2 small red onions, cut into wedges

12 black olives, pitted

1 teaspoon dried oregano

a small bunch of basil

FOR THE VINAIGRETTE

1 garlic clove, chopped finely

juice and zest of 1 lemon or

1 tablespoon white wine vinegar

salt and freshly ground black pepper

1 Put all the salad ingredients except the basil into a large bowl.

2 Whisk together the vinaigrette ingredients and 2 tablespoons of water.

3 Pour the dressing over the salad and gently toss together. Serve scattered with the basil.

VEGETABLE AND HERB SALAD WITH TOASTED BREAD
Fattoush

POINTS	
per recipe: 5½	per serving: 1½

ⓥ Serves 4
Preparation and cooking time:
15 minutes
Calories per serving: 155
Freezing: not recommended

This Lebanese recipe is a good way to use up stale bread, especially pitta bread.

2 medium pitta breads

8 Cos lettuce leaves, washed

½ cucumber, cut lengthways into quarters then diced

2 medium, ripe tomatoes, diced

½ red or orange pepper, de-seeded and diced

a bunch of watercress, chopped roughly

a bunch of mint, chopped

FOR THE DRESSING

juice of ½ lemon

2 tablespoons low-fat plain yogurt or virtually fat-free fromage frais

1 tablespoon French or whole-grain mustard

salt and freshly ground black pepper

1 Toast the bread in the toaster or under the grill, then cut into small squares.

2 Place two Cos leaves on each serving plate. Put all the other salad ingredients including the bread into a large bowl.

3 Whisk together all the dressing ingredients. Pour over the salad and toss together. Spoon on to the Cos leaves and serve.

SPINACH AND TURKEY SALAD

POINTS	
per recipe: 7	per serving: 1½

Serves 4
Preparation and cooking time:
10 minutes
Calories per serving: 145
Freezing: not recommended

4 medium slices of bread, cubed

6 turkey rashers, cut crossways to make thin, short strips

225 g (8 oz) baby spinach, washed and dried

12 cherry tomatoes

FOR THE DRESSING

1 tablespoon balsamic vinegar

1 teaspoon French mustard

salt and freshly ground black pepper

1 Toast the bread cubes on a baking tray by placing them under the grill and toasting them on one side; then turn them over and toast again on the other side until golden all round.

2 Dry-fry the turkey rashers in a non-stick frying pan for 2 minutes, until golden.

3 Meanwhile, put the spinach and tomatoes into serving bowls and sprinkle over the turkey rashers and the croûtons.

4 Whisk the dressing ingredients and 2 tablespoons of water together in a bowl, pour over the salad and serve.

GRILLED HALOUMI ON SALAD LEAVES

POINTS	
per recipe: 12½	per serving: 3

ⓥ Serves 4
Preparation time: 15 minutes
Calories per serving: 165
Freezing: not recommended

Haloumi is a Cypriot cheese which has a distinctive elastic texture and salty taste. It is at its best when grilled but must be eaten immediately as it quickly becomes rubbery.

80 g (3 oz) haloumi cheese, sliced into 8 thin slices

4 medium slices of wholemeal bread, toasted on one side under the grill

180 g (6½ oz) bag of mixed salad leaves

FOR THE DRESSING

2 teaspoons olive oil

juice and zest of 1 lemon

1 sprig of rosemary, chopped finely

1 small bunch of parsley, chopped finely

1 garlic clove, crushed

1 Put two slices of haloumi on to the untoasted side of each slice of bread and then grill for 1 or 2 minutes until golden and bubbling. Cut each slice of bread into four.

2 Divide the salad leaves between four serving plates, whisk together the dressing ingredients and then spoon over the salads.

3 Top the salads with the grilled cheese croûtons and eat immediately.

Vegetable and Herb Salad with Toasted Bread: Full of sublimely refreshing flavour.

**Ratatouille:
Delicious and
versatile, this
is wonderful
with pasta,
meat or fish.**

vegetables

The farmers' market is still a part of everyday life in the Mediterranean and people buy fresh vegetables daily on their way to or from work. The recipes in this chapter all use ingredients commonly available in the supermarket and although they are meant to be accompaniments, they could also be enjoyed as light meals.

RATATOUILLE

POINTS

per recipe: 0   per serving: 0

Ⓥ Serves 4

Preparation time: 15 minutes +
30 minutes draining
Calories per serving: 55
Freezing: not recommended

1 large aubergine
2 courgettes
low-fat cooking spray
1 large onion, sliced
2 garlic cloves, chopped
1 green pepper, de-seeded and sliced
200 g can of chopped tomatoes
a bunch of basil
salt and freshly ground black pepper

1 Slice the aubergines and courgettes. Sprinkle them with salt and leave them in a colander for at least 30 minutes. Rinse and then pat dry.

2 Spray a large pan with the cooking spray, then fry the onion, with a couple of tablespoons of water if it sticks, for 4 minutes. Add the garlic and cook for 1 minute.

3 Add the aubergine, courgette, green pepper and seasoning. Cover and simmer for 40 minutes.

4 Add the tomatoes and basil and simmer, uncovered, for 20 minutes.

GREEK POTATO PATTIES
Potato Kephtedes

POINTS

per recipe: 12   per serving: 3

Ⓥ Serves 4

Preparation time: 30 minutes + chilling
Cooking time: 40 minutes
Calories per serving: 235
Freezing: not recommended

These spicy Greek patties are delicious served with Yogurt and Cucumber Dip (page 13).

750 g (1lb 10 oz) potatoes, peeled and chopped
low-fat cooking spray
a bunch of spring onions, sliced finely
1 red chilli, de-seeded and chopped finely
1 tablespoon olive oil
1 egg, beaten
a small bunch of mint, chopped roughly
salt and freshly ground black pepper

1 Bring a large pan of water to the boil and then cook the potatoes for 20 minutes or until tender. Drain, then mash and season.

2 Spray a large frying pan with the cooking spray, then sauté the onions and chilli for 2 minutes. Add a tablespoon of water if they stick.

3 Mix the onions and chilli together with the olive oil, egg and mint into the potato. Season and leave to cool for 20 minutes.

4 Preheat the grill to medium and shape the potato mixture into 8 patties. Place on a foil-lined grill pan.

5 Grill the patties for 5 minutes on each side or until golden.

Greek Potato Patties: Delicious with Roasted Pepper Salad (page 24).

GREEK STUFFED TOMATOES AND PEPPERS

POINTS

per recipe: 10   per serving: 5

Ⓥ Serves 2

Preparation time: 25 minutes

Cooking time: 45 minutes

Calories per serving: 565

Freezing: not recommended

The practice of stuffing vegetables is very popular all over the Mediterranean but especially in Greece.

115 g (4 oz) brown rice, rinsed

1 tablespoon pine kernels

low-fat cooking spray

2 large onions, chopped finely

2 garlic cloves, chopped

50 g (1³/₄ oz) currants

juice and zest of 1 lemon

4 large tomatoes

4 large peppers

2 tablespoons fresh breadcrumbs

salt and freshly ground black pepper

TO SERVE

a small bunch of flat leaf parsley, chopped

a small bunch of coriander or mint, chopped

1 Cook the rice in plenty of boiling water for 30 minutes and then drain. Place in a large bowl.

2 Meanwhile, toast the pine kernels by dry-frying them in a frying pan until golden brown.

3 Spray a frying pan with the cooking spray and sauté the onions and garlic for 4 minutes, adding a couple of tablespoons of water if they stick. Add to the rice in the bowl.

4 Add the currants and lemon juice and zest to the bowl. Season and toss together.

5 Preheat the oven to Gas Mark 4/ 180°C/350°F. Cut a round from the top of each tomato, spoon out the flesh with a teaspoon and add to the stuffing mix. Do the same with the peppers, discarding the seeds. Place the tomatoes and peppers side by side, closely packed together in a baking tin.

6 Spoon the stuffing into the peppers and tomatoes, sprinkle over the breadcrumbs and replace the lids.

7 Bake for 15 minutes and serve with the herbs as a garnish.

VARIATION You could also stuff courgettes or aubergines with the same mixture, adding chopped, dried apricots or prunes instead of the currants and using basil or fresh marjoram instead of the parsley or mint. Adjust the Points accordingly.

SICILIAN AUBERGINES
Caponata

POINTS

per recipe: 5¹/₂   per serving: 1¹/₂

Ⓥ Serves 4

Preparation time: 10 minutes + cooling time

Cooking time: 45 minutes

Calories per serving: 150

Freezing: not recommended

Here is a delicious low-fat version of a dish which creates something wonderful from aubergines. Serve with grilled fish or chicken or baked potatoes adding the Points as necessary.

2 tablespoons pine kernels

low-fat cooking spray

1 onion, sliced finely

500 g (1 lb 2 oz) aubergines, diced small

1 teaspoon dried oregano or

1 tablespoon chopped fresh oregano

400 g can of tomatoes

1 tablespoon honey

50 g (1³/₄ oz) green or black olives, stoned and chopped roughly

3 tablespoons capers, rinsed

1 tablespoon red wine vinegar

salt and freshly ground black pepper

1 Toast the pine kernels in a dry frying pan until golden brown. Spray a large frying pan with the cooking spray and fry the onion for about 4 minutes until soft. Add the

aubergines and oregano and cook, turning frequently, for 5 minutes.

2 Add all the remaining ingredients, except the pine kernels. Cover and simmer for 35 minutes.

3 Taste and adjust the seasoning, adding more vinegar or honey if necessary to achieve a good sweet-and-sour balance.

4 For the best flavour, allow the caponata to cool to room temperature and then scatter over the pine kernels just before serving.

COOK'S TIP Caponata tastes even better if it is left overnight in the fridge and then brought back to room temperature again before serving.

Sicilian Aubergines: A medley of some of the most delicious Mediterranean ingredients.

Bulgar Wheat Pilaff: A traditional Turkish dish.

ROASTED ASPARAGUS WITH A LEMON DRESSING

POINTS

per recipe: $4\frac{1}{2}$ per serving: 1

Ⓥ *if using vegetarian parmesan*
Serves 4
Preparation time: 5 minutes
Cooking time: 20 minutes
Calories per serving: 65
Freezing: not recommended

---

700 g (1 lb 9 oz) asparagus spears
2 teaspoons olive oil
juice of 2 lemons
25 g (1 oz) parmesan cheese shavings
salt and freshly ground black pepper
4 lemon wedges, to serve

---

1 Preheat the oven to Gas Mark 6/ 200°C/400°F. Trim the asparagus spears of their woody ends and place in a shallow roasting tray.
2 Pour over the olive oil and lemon juice. Season and toss the spears before putting them in the oven for 20 minutes, until just tender.
3 Sprinkle with parmesan shavings, and serve with lemon wedges.

COOK'S TIPS The cooking time in this recipe applies to asparagus of a medium thickness and so should be adjusted if you're using very thick or thin stems.

An easy way to get nice parmesan shavings is to use a potato peeler.

VARIATION Use 2 tablespoons of balsamic vinegar in step 2 instead of lemon juice.

TURKISH RICE PILAFF

POINTS

per recipe: $12\frac{1}{2}$ per serving: 3

Serves 4
Preparation time: 10 minutes
Cooking time: 15 minutes
Calories per serving: 240
Freezing: not recommended

This Turkish dish is enjoyed everywhere in the Mediterranean.

---

250 g (9 oz) long grain rice
low-fat cooking spray
1 small onion, chopped finely
1.2 litres (2 pints) chicken stock
sea salt and freshly ground black pepper

---

1 Wash the rice, then drain. Spray a large saucepan with the cooking spray and fry the onion for 4 minutes. Then add the rice and cook over a low heat, stirring, for 2 minutes until opaque.

2 Add the stock and seasoning, bring it to the boil and then stir. Reduce the heat, cover and simmer for about 15 minutes, until the stock has been absorbed and holes appear on the surface of the rice.
3 Remove from the heat and let stand, covered for 5 minutes. Fluff up with a fork and transfer to a serving dish.

VARIATION It's far more nutritious, satisfying and delicious to use brown rice but then you must increase the cooking time to 30 minutes.

BULGAR WHEAT PILAFF

POINTS

per recipe: $18\frac{1}{2}$ per serving: $4\frac{1}{2}$

Serves 4
Preparation time: 5 minutes
Cooking time: 20 minutes +
10 minutes standing time
Calories per serving: 315
Freezing: not recommended

Bulgar wheat has a satisfying texture and makes an interesting change from potatoes or rice.

---

25 g (1 oz) pine kernels
25 g (1 oz) flaked almonds
low-fat cooking spray
1 onion
225 g (8 oz) bulgar wheat
600 ml (1 pint) chicken stock
50 g (1¾ oz) raisins, sultanas or currants
a small bunch of coriander or mint, chopped
salt and freshly ground black pepper

---

1 Toast the pine kernels and almonds in a dry frying pan. Spray a pan with the cooking oil and fry the onion for 4 minutes or until soft. Add a tablespoon of water if it sticks.
2 Stir in the bulgar wheat and cook for a further 4 minutes, stirring all the time. Add the stock, bring to the boil and stir. Then reduce the heat, cover and simmer for 20 minutes until all the liquid is absorbed.
3 Season, add the other ingredients and place a sheet of baking parchment over the pan. Replace the lid and allow to stand for 10 minutes. Fluff up with a fork before serving.

vegetarian meals

Vegetables have always been an important part of the Mediterranean diet but more recently we have been including more fresh vegetables and fruit in our diet in Britain. Healthy vegetarian meals are not just for vegetarians anymore; they make satisfying and delicious meals for everyone.

RICOTTA-STUFFED MUSHROOMS

POINTS

per recipe: 9½   per serving: 2½

 Serves 4

*Preparation time: 5 minutes +
10 minutes soaking
Cooking time: 20 minutes
Calories per serving: 110
Freezing: not recommended*

You'll need large, flat open mushrooms for this Italian recipe. Serve with a fresh salad and some crusty bread, adding the Points as necessary.

4 halves of sun-dried tomatoes, from a packet

*8 large flat mushrooms (about 450 g/ 1 lb), stalks removed and chopped
low-fat cooking spray
½ onion, chopped
2 garlic cloves, crushed
a small bunch of parsley, chopped
100 g (3½ oz) fresh wholemeal breadcrumbs
75 g (2¾ oz) ricotta cheese*

1 Preheat the oven to Gas Mark 4/ 180°C/350°F. Soak the sun-dried tomatoes in 2 tablespoons of warm water for 10 minutes. Place the mushrooms on a large baking tray.
2 Spray a frying pan with the cooking spray and fry the onion until soft, about 4 minutes. Add water if it

sticks. Then add the garlic and cook for a further minute.
3 In a bowl, mix together the cooked onions, garlic, mushroom stalks, parsley, breadcrumbs and cheese. Reserve the soaking liquid and chop the soaked tomatoes.
4 Add the tomatoes and soaking liquid to the stuffing mixture and then spoon it into the mushrooms. Bake for 15 minutes.

VARIATIONS Spoon the stuffing into courgettes or sweet peppers and cook for 35–40 minutes or spoon into marrow and cook for 45 minutes. You could also use large tomatoes; cook them for 15–20 minutes.

ITALIAN BAKED COURGETTES

POINTS

per recipe: 8½   per serving: 2

 Serves 4

*Preparation time: 15 minutes
Cooking time: 25 minutes
Calories per serving: 165
Freezing: not recommended*

*2 medium slices of wholewheat bread
700 g (1 lb 9 oz) courgettes
2 eggs, beaten
4 tablespoons skimmed milk*

*100 ml (3½ fl oz) low-fat plain yogurt
100 g (3½ oz) low-fat soft cheese
a small bunch of fresh marjoram
sea salt and freshly ground black pepper*

1 Preheat the grill to high. Process the bread to crumbs in a food processor.
2 Slice the courgettes diagonally into 1 cm (½-inch) thick, long slices and lay them on a large baking sheet. Place under the grill for 5 minutes or until blackening at the edges and slightly dried out.

3 Preheat the oven to Gas Mark 5/ 190°C/375°F. Place a layer of courgettes in the bottom of an ovenproof dish and then scatter with one-third of the marjoram.
4 Beat together the eggs, milk, yogurt, cheese and seasoning. Pour one-third of this mixture over the courgettes and marjoram. Repeat with another layer until all the courgettes and marjoram are used up.
5 Sprinkle the top layer with breadcrumbs and bake for 25 minutes or until the top is golden.

Ricotta-Stuffed Mushrooms: Stuffing vegetables is very popular in the Mediterranean and it's a good way to bulk them out.

Greek Spinach and Filo Pie: One of Greece's most popular dishes.

GREEK SPINACH AND FILO PIE
Spanakopitta

POINTS

per recipe: 9½	per serving: 2½

 Serves 4

Preparation time: 30 minutes
Cooking time: 45 minutes
Calories per serving: 235
Freezing: not recommended

This Greek dish is now popular all over the Mediterranean.

500 g (1 lb 2 oz) spinach, washed, tough stems removed and chopped
low-fat cooking spray
1 onion, chopped finely
a bunch of spring onions, chopped finely, including the green tops
a small bunch of flat leaf parsley, chopped finely
a small bunch of dill, chopped finely
¼ teaspoon grated nutmeg
100 g (3½ oz) low-fat soft cheese
100 g (3½ oz) plain cottage cheese
8 sheets of filo pastry
salt and freshly ground black pepper

1 Preheat the oven to Gas Mark 3/ 170°C/320°F. Place the wet spinach in a saucepan with the lid on and cook for 4 minutes until completely wilted. Transfer to a colander and press down with a wooden spoon to extract the moisture. Then put it in a large bowl.

2 Spray a frying pan with the cooking spray and sauté the onion for 5 minutes, stirring occasionally. Add the spring onions and cook for a further 2 minutes. Add them to the spinach with the herbs, seasoning and cheeses. Beat everything together with a wooden spoon.

3 Spray a metal 23 cm (9-inch) square baking tin or ovenproof dish with the cooking spray. Fit the bottom of the tray with 5 sheets of pastry, one on top of the other, spraying each with a little olive oil as you lay them down, and folding them up and over the sides of the dish.

4 Spread the spinach mixture over the filo, then cover with the remaining 5 sheets, spraying the cooking oil between each layer as well as on top.

5 Score through the top sheets of pastry with a knife to make diamond shaped portions which will make cutting them up easier later (cut diagonally to the right and then to the left). Sprinkle with a little water to prevent the pastry curling and brush lightly to spread the water evenly.

6 Bake for 45 minutes until golden and crispy. Allow to stand for a few minutes before cutting into portions and serving.

SPINACH CANNELLONI

POINTS

per recipe: 16	per serving: 4

 Serves 4

Preparation time: 25 minutes
Cooking time: 45 minutes
Calories per serving: 445
Freezing: not recommended

This delicious recipe has been adapted from the classic Italian dish.

400 g (14 oz) spinach
low-fat cooking spray
1 onion, chopped finely
2 garlic cloves, chopped finely
¼ teaspoon grated nutmeg
a bunch of basil, chopped roughly
16 quick-cook cannelloni tubes
salt and freshly ground black pepper
a few fresh basil leaves, to garnish
1 tablespoon grated parmesan cheese

FOR THE TOPPING

2 teaspoons cornflour mixed with
1 tablespoon water
450 ml (16 fl oz) low-fat plain yogurt
100 g (3½ oz) low-fat soft cheese

1 Wash the spinach and put in a large saucepan with the lid on. Cook gently for 10 minutes, stirring occasionally until wilted but not dry.

2 Preheat the oven to Gas Mark 4/ 180°C/350°F. Spray a pan with the cooking spray and sauté the onion and garlic gently for 4 minutes or until softened, adding a tablespoon of water if it sticks.

3 Add the spinach, nutmeg and most of the basil. Mix together. Put this mixture to one side to cool a little.

4 Beat together the topping ingredients to obtain a thick and creamy consistency. Season to taste.

5 Stuff the cannelloni with the spinach mixture using a teaspoon. Put in an ovenproof dish tightly packed together. Spoon over the topping and sprinkle with the parmesan.

6 Bake for 45 minutes until the top is golden and the cannelloni cooked. Sprinkle with fresh basil leaves.

COOK'S TIP Instead of fresh spinach, you could use defrosted, frozen spinach. There is no need to blanch it, just squeeze out any excess water and chop it.

VEGETABLE COUSCOUS WITH HARISSA

POINTS

per recipe: 25½   per serving: 6½

 Serves 4

Preparation time: 20 minutes

Cooking time: 30 minutes

Calories per serving: 560

Freezing: not recommended

450 g (1 lb) quick-cook couscous

low-fat cooking spray

2 onions, quartered

225 g (8 oz) pumpkin, seeds removed, peeled and diced

225 g (8 oz) carrots, peeled and sliced

2 garlic cloves, crushed

a pinch of saffron strands

2 cinnamon sticks

2 tablespoons coriander seeds, crushed

1 teaspoon paprika

1 red chilli

225 g (8 oz) tomatoes

225 g (8 oz) courgettes

50 g (1¾ oz) raisins

175 g (6 oz) shellled fresh or frozen broad beans

450 ml (16 fl oz) vegetable stock

1 bunch of fresh coriander, chopped roughly, to garnish

sea salt and freshly ground pepper

FOR THE HARISSA

2 tablespoons tomato purée

1 garlic clove, crushed

1 teaspoon cayenne pepper

1 teaspoon ground coriander

1 teaspoon ground cumin

4 mint sprigs, chopped finely

1 Put the couscous in a bowl and pour over enough boiling water to cover it plus 2.5 cm (1 inch). Cover the whole bowl with a plate or clingfilm and leave to steam.

2 Spray a large pan with the cooking spray, then sauté the onions for 4 minutes, adding a tablespoon of water if they stick. Add the pumpkin, carrots and garlic and cook for another 3 minutes. Add the saffron, cinnamon, coriander, paprika and whole chilli. Lower the heat, cover and cook for 5 minutes.

3 Meanwhile, chop the tomatoes into small dice and cut the courgettes into thick slices. Add to the pan with the raisins, broad beans and stock. Season and then cook uncovered for 20 minutes. Stir frequently until the vegetables are tender and the stock has been reduced and thickened.

4 Make the harissa by mixing together all the ingredients, then add 4 tablespoons of the liquid from the stew.

5 Remove the plate or clingfilm from the couscous and fluff up with a fork. Put on serving plates. Remove the cinnamon sticks from the stew and then spoon the stew over the couscous. Serve with the harissa and sprinkle with fresh coriander.

COOK'S TIP You could also buy the Bart Spice harissa mixture. The Points per tablespoon will be 1.

VEGETABLE LASAGNE

POINTS

per recipe: 22   per serving: 5½

 Serves 4

Preparation time: 15 minutes

Cooking time: 40 minutes

Calories per serving: 455

Freezing: recommended

Here is a low-fat version of lasagne with the traditional béchamel sauce.

low-fat cooking spray

2 large onions, sliced

2 garlic cloves, chopped finely

225 g (8 oz) mushrooms, sliced

225 g (8 oz) courgettes, sliced into rounds

225 g (8 oz) broccoli, cut into small florets

1 bay leaf

a bunch of thyme, woody stems removed, chopped

1 quantity of Italian tomato sauce (page 9)

250 g (9 oz) ready-to-cook lasagne sheets, preferably spinach

4 teaspoons grated parmesan cheese

salt and freshly ground black pepper

FOR THE TOPPING

2 eggs

4 tablespoons skimmed milk

300 ml (½ pint) low-fat plain yogurt

100 g (3½ oz) low-fat soft cheese

1 Preheat the oven to Gas Mark 6/ 200°C/400°F. Spray a large frying pan with the cooking spray, then sauté the onions and garlic for 4 minutes, adding 2 tablespoons of water if they stick. Then add the mushrooms, courgettes, broccoli, herbs and seasoning. Cook for a further 4 minutes with the lid on. Lastly, stir in the tomato sauce.

2 Spray a 30 cm (12-inch) ovenproof dish with the cooking spray, then line it with lasagne sheets. Spoon over a layer of the mixture. Lay the rest of the lasagne sheets on top and the rest of the mixture on top of that.

3 Make the cheese sauce by beating together the eggs, milk, yogurt and soft cheese. Season and then pour over the top of the lasagne. Sprinkle with the parmesan and bake in the oven for 40 minutes, until golden.

Vegetable Couscous with Harissa: Couscous is a staple in North Africa and harissa is a spicy purée of chillies, garlic, coriander seeds and cumin.

Paella: Rice and saffron are the only really essential ingredients in this dish so there's lots of room for creativity!

fish & seafood

One of the reasons the Mediterranean diet is so healthy, is that it includes so much fish and seafood.

PAELLA

POINTS	
per recipe: 23	per serving: 5½

Serves 4
Preparation time: 10 minutes
Cooking time: 35 minutes
Calories per serving: 435
Freezing: not recommended

low-fat cooking spray
2 medium chicken breasts, skinned and cut into bite-sized pieces
1 onion, chopped
1 red pepper, de-seeded and chopped
3 garlic cloves, crushed
3 ripe tomatoes, chopped
a generous pinch of saffron
2 teaspoons paprika
a small bunch of thyme, woody stems removed and then chopped
250 g (9 oz) rice, preferably brown or long-grain and wild mix
1.2 litres (2 pints) chicken stock
400 g (14 oz) frozen seafood, defrosted
125 g (4½ oz) frozen peas
lemon wedges, to serve
salt and freshly ground black pepper

1 Spray a large pan with the cooking spray, then sauté the chicken pieces for 5 minutes. Stir frequently and season, then remove from the pan to a plate and leave to one side.

2 Spray the pan again with the cooking spray, then put the onion, red pepper and garlic in the pan. Stir-fry for 4 minutes or until softened and then add the tomatoes, saffron, paprika and thyme. Cook for a further 2 minutes.

3 Add the rice and stir until well mixed, then add half the stock. Bring to a simmer and cook for 10 minutes. Then add the rest of the stock and the chicken and cook for a further 10 minutes without stirring. Lastly, add the seafood and the peas. Stir once, gently, and finish cooking for 5 minutes or until the rice is tender.

4 Taste to check the seasoning and serve with lemon wedges.

GARLIC PRAWNS

POINTS	
per recipe: 9½	per serving: 2½

Serves 4
Preparation and cooking time: 10 minutes
Calories per serving: 180
Freezing: not recommended

low-fat cooking spray
3 garlic cloves, sliced thinly
1 red chilli, de-seeded and chopped finely (optional)
400 g (14 oz) large, frozen, cooked and peeled prawns
a small bunch of parsley, chopped
juice of 1 lemon
salt
4 medium slices of crusty bread, to serve

1 Spray a large frying pan with the cooking spray, then add the garlic and chilli, if using. Stir-fry for 2 minutes. Add the prawns and 4 tablespoons of water. Sprinkle with a little salt.

2 Stir-fry for another 3 or 4 minutes, then add the chopped parsley. Squeeze over the lemon juice and then spoon on to serving plates. Serve with the bread to mop up the juices.

Garlic Prawns: One of Spain's most popular tapas dishes.

150g (5½ oz) frozen tiger prawns without shells, defrosted
250 g (9 oz) frozen seafood, defrosted
a bunch of flat leaf parsley, chopped
salt and freshly ground black pepper

1 Spray a large pan with the cooking spray and sauté the onion for 4 minutes adding 1–2 tablespoons of water if it sticks. Add the garlic and fennel or celery and cook for a further 10 minutes. Then add the tomatoes, thyme, bay leaf, orange juice and zest, lemon zest, and the saffron. Stir together.

2 Add the stock and bring to the boil, then simmer for 20 minutes, uncovered. Add the fish, prawns and seafood. Season and cook for a final 3 minutes.

3 Stir in the fresh parsley, check the seasoning and then serve.

COOK'S TIP To make your own fish stock, use the trimmings, bones or prawn shells from any fish or seafood you have or ask the fishmonger for some trimmings. Put them in a pan with ½ an onion, a handful of parsley stalks, a bay leaf and a few peppercorns. Add water to cover, bring to a boil and then simmer, uncovered for 20 minutes. Strain and use as required or store, covered, in the fridge for up to 4 days.

Mediterranean Fish Stew: This is a regular feature on menus in the Mediterranean.

MEDITERRANEAN FISH STEW

POINTS

per recipe: 7½	per serving: 2

Serves 4
Preparation time: 10 minutes
Cooking time: 35 minutes
Calories per serving: 185
Freezing: not recommended

This recipe uses widely available fish and seafood coupled with the vibrant flavours of aniseed and citrus. Don't be put off by the large amount of garlic which is absolutely delicious in this stew!

low-fat cooking spray
1 onion, chopped finely
4 garlic cloves, chopped finely
1 small fennel bulb, chopped finely or 8 sticks celery, chopped finely
400 g can of chopped tomatoes
a small bunch of thyme, woody stems removed
1 bay leaf
juice and grated zest of 1 orange
grated zest of ½ lemon
a pinch of saffron strands
700 ml (1¼ pint) fish or vegetable stock (see Cook's Tip)
250 g (9 oz) thick cod or coley fillet, cut into bite-sized cubes

BAKED COD IN A PARCEL

POINTS

per recipe: 11   **per serving:** 2½

Serves 4
Preparation time: 10 minutes
Cooking time: 20 minutes
Calories per serving: 210
Freezing: not recommended

The advantage of cooking fish in baking parchment is that the fish cooks quickly and seals in all the flavours. Also, opening the parcels up, as you do in this Portuguese recipe, is an exciting way to start a meal

4 cod fillets (each about 175 g/6 oz), skinned
1 red pepper, de-seeded and diced finely
1 red onion, diced finely
a small bunch of fresh oregano, chopped
2 garlic cloves, chopped finely
2 tomatoes, chopped
juice of 1 lemon
1 tablespoon olive oil
4 tablespoons dry white wine or balsamic vinegar
salt and freshly ground black pepper

1 Preheat the oven to Gas Mark 6/ 200°C/400°F. Cut 4 sheets of non-stick baking parchment to measure 30 × 30 cm (12 × 12 inches). Place a piece of fish in the middle of each piece of paper diagonally from corner to corner.

2 In a bowl, mix together the pepper, onion, oregano, garlic, tomatoes, lemon juice, olive oil and wine or vinegar. Season well with salt and pepper.

3 Spoon the mixture on top of the fish. Fold the parchment over the fish to form a triangle. Fold the edges together tightly to form a sealed parcel.

4. Lift the parcels on to a baking sheet and bake for 15–20 minutes. Place each parcel on a plate and serve at once, allowing each guest to experience the cloud of fragrant steam which emerges from the parcels.

VARIATION This dish is equally delicious with trout (4 Points per serving), salmon (5 Points per serving) or seabass (3 Points per serving). With haddock, coley and monkfish, the Points will remain the same. Just use what is freshest at the supermarket.

SPICY GRILLED SARDINES

POINTS

per recipe: 19½   **per serving:** 5

Serves 4
Preparation and cooking time:
10 minutes
Calories per serving: 145
Freezing: not recommended

This is the sort of dish which is popular in coastal villages all around the Mediterranean. Serve with couscous and salad, toast or Italian Garlic Toasts (page 16) adding extra Points as necessary.

4 garlic cloves, crushed
½ teaspoon paprika
1 teaspoon ground cumin
1 tablespoon lemon juice
2 teaspoons olive oil
12–16 (about 600 g/1 lb 5 oz) fresh sardines, cleaned
salt and freshly ground black pepper

1 Mix the garlic with the spices, lemon juice, olive oil and seasoning. Brush this mixture all over the sardines to coat thoroughly.

2 Heat the grill and place the sardines on a rack over the grill pan. Grill for approximately 2 minutes on each side until cooked through.

COOK'S TIP One of the easiest ways to make this paste is to put all the ingredients in a pestle and mortar with the whole garlic cloves and pulvarise together.

VARIATION This recipe can be made with canned sardines in brine in exactly the same way, although the cooking time can be reduced to a minute on each side as the fish is already cooked and just needs to be warmed through. This could also be done in a frying pan. The Points will remain the same.

MOULES PROVENÇALES

POINTS

per recipe: 4	per serving: ½

Serves 4
Preparation time: 10 minutes
Cooking time: 15 minutes
Calories per serving: 125
Freezing: not recommended

Serve with crusty bread to mop up the juice adding the extra Points.

---

low-fat cooking spray
2 garlic cloves, chopped finely
1 onion, chopped finely
150 ml (¼ pint) stock
400 g can of chopped tomatoes
a bunch of fresh basil or thyme, chopped
1 kg (2 lb 4 oz) washed mussels
salt and freshly ground black pepper

1 Spray a large saucepan with the cooking spray, then sauté the garlic and onion for 5 minutes until soft, adding a little water if necessary.

2 Add the stock, tomatoes, herbs and seasoning. Cook briskly for 5 minutes. Then add the mussels and put the lid on the pan. Continue to cook for another 5 minutes, shaking the pan vigorously a few times.

3 When you remove the lid, the mussels should have opened. Any that have not opened, should be discarded. Spoon into serving bowls.

VARIATION Replace the stock with white wine. Points per serving are 1.

GRILLED FISH WITH A SPICY MOROCCAN SAUCE
Chermoula

POINTS

per recipe: 8½	per serving: 2

Serves 4
Preparation time: 5 minutes
Cooking time: 15 minutes
Calories per serving: 150
Freezing: not recommended

---

4 cod fish steaks, each weighing about 175 g/6 oz
salt and freshly ground black pepper

FOR THE CHERMOULA
a small bunch of fresh coriander, chopped roughly
a small bunch of fresh mint, chopped
2 garlic cloves, chopped
1 red chilli, de-seeded and chopped
1 teaspoon paprika
2 teaspoons cumin seeds, toasted in a dry frying pan for 2 minutes
a pinch of saffron

1–2 tablespoons low-fat fromage frais or yogurt
juice of 1 lemon
salt

1 Preheat the grill to high. Place the fish steaks on the grill rack and season. Grill for 6–8 minutes on each side or until lighly browned and cooked through.

2 Mix all the chermoula ingredients together in a bowl. Then spoon over the hot fish and serve.

SPANISH FISH AND POTATO BAKE

POINTS

per recipe: 15½	per serving: 4

Serves 4
Preparation time: 35 minutes
Cooking time: 20 minutes
Calories per serving: 330
Freezing: not recommended

This tasty bake makes a lovely family meal with its sweet onions and crispy top. Serve with salad.

---

450 g (1 lb) thick cod fillets
low-fat cooking spray
3 large onions, sliced thinly
3 garlic cloves, chopped finely
900 g (2 lb) potatoes, unpeeled
a small bunch of flat leaf parsley, chopped
150 ml (¼ pint) fish or chicken stock
salt and freshly ground black pepper
a small handful of flat leaf parsley, to garnish

1 Preheat the oven to Gas Mark 4/ 180°C/350°F. Place the fish fillets on a lightly oiled baking tray. Spray with the cooking spray and bake for 10 minutes.

2 Meanwhile, spray a frying pan with the cooking spray and sauté the onions for about 20 minutes. Add a tablespoon of water if they stick, and cook until golden brown. Add the garlic and sauté for 2 more minutes.

3 Meanwhile, boil the potatoes until tender. Drain and leave to cool slightly, then peel and cut into 1 cm (½-inch) slices.

4 Separate the fish into large flakes. Spray a large oval ovenproof dish with the cooking spray and layer the potatoes, onions, parsley and fish in the dish, seasoning each layer. Pour over the stock and bake for 20 minutes. Serve garnished with parsley.

VARIATION Garnish with 4 hard-boiled eggs as well. Add 1½ Points per serving.

Moules Provençales: Here's how the French like to enjoy mussels while relaxing in the sunny South of France.

The land in the Mediterranean is not ideal for grazing large herds, especially cattle, and so meat is rare which makes it highly prized. The scarcity of meat also means that recipes are made more filling with pulses and nuts and/or fruit. Poultry, however, is everywhere and enjoyed in so many unique and interesting ways.

CHICKEN KEBABS

POINTS

per recipe: 20½   **per serving: 5**

Serves 4
Preparation and cooking time:
25 minutes
Calories per serving: 355
Freezing: not recommended

This classic Greek recipe can either be cooked under the grill or on the barbecue.

400 g (14 oz) skinless chicken breast, cubed
4 red onions, cut into wedges
4 red peppers, de-seeded and cut into squares
8 bay leaves
1 lemon, cut into wedges
4 medium pitta breads
FOR THE MARINADE
1 garlic clove, chopped
2 tablespoons low-fat plain yogurt
1 tablespoon clear honey
1 tablespoon soy sauce
2 tablespoons red wine vinegar or lemon juice

1 Preheat the grill to medium. Mix all the marinade ingredients together in a bowl.

2 Thread the chicken, onions, red peppers, bay leaves and lemon wedges on to 8 skewers.

3 Brush the kebabs with the marinade, reserving a little to serve with, and grill for about 10 minutes. Turn the kebabs at least once, until golden and cooked through. Meanwhile, warm the pitta breads under the grill.

4 Serve in the warmed pitta breads, with the reserved marinade poured over the top.

COOK'S TIP If you are using wooden skewers, soak them in water for 10 minutes or so before threading the meat on to them to prevent them from burning.

VARIATIONS Kebabs are great made from pork or beef or even firm fish like monkfish or scallops. Instead of serving this in pitta bread, you could serve it with rice, adjusting the Points as necessary.

Chicken Kebabs: Delicious served with Bulgar Wheat Pilaff, (page 35).

MOROCCAN CHICKEN TAGINE

POINTS

per recipe: **20**   per serving: **5**

Ⓥ *Serves 4*
Preparation time: 5 minutes
Cooking time 1½ hours
Calories per serving: 265
Freezing: not recommended

This North African dish is named after the pot with a tall, conical lid in which it is traditionally cooked. Serve accompanied by rice or couscous, adding extra Points as necessary.

---

4 × 175 g (6 oz) skinless chicken breasts
2 onions, chopped
2 cinnamon sticks
½ teaspoon ground ginger
½ teaspoon ground coriander
250 g (9 oz) prunes (either canned in prune juice or dried and soaked overnight)
1 tablespoon honey
salt

1 Put the chicken in a large pan with the chopped onions and cinnamon sticks. Sprinkle with the ginger, coriander and salt, to taste, and then cover with water. Simmer gently, covered, for 1 hour.

2 Add the prunes and the honey and cook for a further ½ hour, uncovered, until the prunes are soft and the sauce reduced considerably.

VARIATION Instead of prunes, you can use apricots or fresh cooking apple; just remember to adjust the Points. If using apple, add it 15 minutes before the end of the cooking time. It's best to use cooking apples because they will not disintegrate as easily when they are cooked.

Rosemary and Lemon Chicken: Enjoy the tastes and aromas of Italy.

ROSEMARY AND LEMON CHICKEN

POINTS

per recipe: **30½**   per serving: **7½**

Serves 4
Preparation time: 25 minutes
Cooking time 30 minutes
Calories per serving: 410
Freezing: not recommended

This is a fantastically fragrant chicken and potato bake from Italy.

---

8 medium skinless, boneless chicken thighs, fat and skin removed, cut into bite-sized pieces
2 unwaxed lemons, halved
950 g (2 lb 2 oz) potatoes, peeled and cut into 4 cm (1½-inch) cubes
6 garlic cloves, halved lengthways
2 onions, sliced
10 rosemary sprigs, 2 reserved for garnishing
low-fat cooking spray
salt and freshly ground black pepper

1 Put the chicken pieces into a bowl and season, then squeeze over the lemon halves. Slice one of the squeezed lemon halves into thin slivers and then add these too.
2 Bring a large pan of water to the boil and blanch the potatoes for 4 minutes only, then drain.
3 Preheat the oven to Gas Mark 7/ 220°C/425°F. Put all the ingredients into a roasting tin, spray with the low-fat cooking spray, lightly season and toss together. Bake for 30 minutes, turning every now and then until crispy and golden and cooked through. Serve garnished with fresh rosemary sprigs.

Moroccan Chicken Tagine: North African cooking is deliciously sweet and savoury at the same time.

Mediterranean
Turkey Rolls:
An elegant dish
for entertaining.

MOROCCAN COUSCOUS

POINTS

per recipe: 19½   per serving: 5

Ⓥ *Serves 4*
Preparation time: 15 minutes
Cooking time 1 hour 10 minutes
Calories per serving: 580
Freezing: not recommended

Couscous is the national dish of Tunisia, Algeria and Morocco. Traditionally, the dish is made with a lamb or chicken and vegetable stew over which the couscous is steamed.

low-fat cooking spray
3 onions, chopped
2 garlic cloves, crushed
2 cinnamon sticks
½ teaspoon tumeric
400 g (14 oz) boned leg of lamb, cubed and fat removed
a small bunch of flat leaf parsley, chopped
a small bunch of coriander, chopped, with some reserved for garnishing
400 g can of chopped tomatoes
400 g can of chick-peas, drained
4 carrots, peeled, quartered lengthways, then cut into thirds to make batons
4 medium parsnips, quartered lengthways, then cut into thirds to make batons
200 g (7 oz) quick-cook couscous
salt and freshly ground black pepper

1 Spray a large saucepan with the cooking spray and sauté the onions, garlic, cinnamon and tumeric together for 5 minutes over a low heat, adding a tablespoon or two of water if they stick. Turn up the heat and add the lamb. Sauté, stirring for 5 minutes or until sealed all over.
2 Add the herbs, tomatoes, 850 ml (1½ pints) water and seasoning.
Reduce the heat, cover and simmer for 30 minutes. Then add the chick-peas, carrots and parsnips and simmer for a further 20 minutes, covered.
3 Turn up the heat and remove the lid. Place the couscous in a sieve and rest over the pan, then cover with foil and seal the edges. Cook the couscous like this for 20 minutes, then turn it out into a bowl and fluff up with a fork.
4 Spoon the stew on top of the couscous and serve sprinkled with some coriander.

VARIATION If you prefer, you can cook the couscous by placing it in a bowl and covering it with 2.5 cm (1 inch) of boiling water. Place a plate over the bowl or cover with foil or clingfilm. Leave for 5 minutes. Remove the lid and fluff up with a fork, then serve.

MEDITERRANEAN TURKEY ROLLS

POINTS

per recipe: 22   per serving: 5½

Ⓥ *Serves 4*
Preparation and cooking time: 45 minutes + cooling
Calories per serving: 205
Freezing: not recommended

Basil complements turkey so well.

2 aubergines
2 red peppers
100 g (3½ oz) ricotta cheese
a large bunch of fresh basil, chopped, with a few chopped leaves reserved
8 thin turkey escalopes (about 400 g/ 14 oz in total)
low-fat cooking spray
1 garlic clove, crushed
2 tablespoons white wine vinegar
400 g can of chopped tomatoes
1 teaspoon clear honey
salt and freshly ground black pepper

1 Preheat the oven to Gas Mark 6/ 200°C/400°F. Place the whole aubergines and red peppers on a baking tray and bake for 20 minutes. Then leave to cool.
2 Meanwhile, put the ricotta in a bowl with half the chopped fresh basil and season. Put the turkey escalopes between two sheets of baking parchment, foil or clingfilm. Season and then beat with a rolling pin or meat-tenderising mallet until thin but not broken.
3 When the peppers are cool enough to handle, peel them and then chop them finely. Mix with the ricotta and remaining basil. Put
spoonfuls of this along one end of the turkey escalopes and then roll them up. Line a baking tray with foil and spray with the cooking spray. Place the rolls on the foil and bake in the oven for 10 minutes until golden and cooked through.
4 In the meantime, slice the aubergines in half lengthwise, scoop out all the flesh and chop well. Spray a frying pan with the cooking spray and sauté the garlic for 2 minutes, then add the white wine vinegar and the aubergine flesh.
5 Cook for 2 minutes, stirring, then add the tomatoes, seasoning, the reserved basil leaves and honey. Cook for 10 minutes. Check the seasoning and then serve poured over the turkey rolls.

1 Sprinkle the aubergines with salt and put in a colander for 15 minutes. Then rinse and dry with a tea towel or kitchen paper. Preheat the grill to high. Place the aubergines on the grill rack, and grill for 2 minutes on each side until lightly browned and dry.

2 Meanwhile, make the meat sauce. Spray a frying pan with the cooking spray and sauté the onion and garlic for 4 minutes, adding a couple of tablespoons of water if they stick. Then add the meat and stir to break up. Cook for 5 minutes or until it is browned all over.

3 Add the remaining ingredients for the meat sauce, and gently simmer, uncovered, for 15 minutes. Then remove the cinnamon stick.

4 Meanwhile, make the béchamel sauce and preheat the oven to Gas Mark 3/170°C/320°F. Melt the margarine, then stir in the flour. Gradually add the milk, stirring or whisking all the time to remove the lumps. Stir in the soft cheese and mustard and season to taste.

5 In a large ovenproof dish, layer the aubergines with the meat sauce, then pour over the cheese sauce. Scatter with the grated cheese and bake for 30 minutes until the top is bubbling and golden.

COOK'S TIP This dish is delicious hot or cold and the flavour improves if left overnight in the refrigerator and heated up the next day.

**Moussaka:
Greek comfort
food.**

MOUSSAKA

POINTS

per recipe: *27*   **per serving:** *6½*

Serves 4

Preparation time: 50 minutes

Cooking time: 30 minutes

Calories per serving: 445

Freezing: not recommended

*600 g (1 lb 5 oz) aubergines, sliced
into 1 cm (½-inch) thick rounds*

FOR THE MEAT SAUCE

low-fat cooking spray

1 onion, chopped roughly

2 garlic cloves, chopped finely

400 g (14 oz) lean minced beef

1 tablespoon Worcestershire sauce

400 g can of chopped tomatoes

*1½ teaspoons ground cinnamon or
2 cinnamon sticks*

a small bunch of parsley, chopped

1 tablespoon clear honey

salt and freshly ground black pepper

FOR THE BÉCHAMEL SAUCE

*2 tablespoons polyunsaturated
margarine*

2 tablespoons wholemeal flour

600 ml (1 pint) skimmed milk

100 g (3½ oz) low-fat soft cheese

1 tablespoon French mustard

*50 g (1¾ oz) half-fat Cheddar cheese,
grated*

GREEK MEAT PATTIES
Keftethes

POINTS

per recipe: 25½   per serving: 6½

Serves 4
Preparation time: 15 minutes
Cooking time 15 minutes
Calories per serving: 350
Freezing: recommended

These patties are delicious with rice and salad, adding extra Points for the rice.

6 medium slices of bread, crusts removed
1 onion, chopped finely
a bunch of flat leaf parsley, chopped finely
a bunch of mint, chopped finely
2 eggs
zest and juice of ½ lemon
300 g (10½ oz) lamb mince
70 g (2½ oz) plain flour
low-fat cooking spray
salt and freshly ground black pepper

1 Soak the bread in a few tablespoons of water and then squeeze dry with your hands. Put the bread in a bowl with all the other ingredients except the flour and cooking spray. Mix to a paste.
2 With moistened hands, shape into 12 burger-shaped patties. Put the flour into a shallow tray and coat the patties in it.
3 Spray a frying pan with the oil and fry the patties in batches for 5 minutes on each side until thoroughly cooked through. Remove and place on kitchen paper to drain off any oil, then serve.

COOK'S TIP Only freeze when raw; do not freeze cooked patties. Also, be sure to defrost thoroughly before cooking.

VARIATIONS Make the patties smaller and serve as a starter or cocktail nibble.

Although it won't be authentically Greek, these patties could also be made with turkey mince for delicious, low-fat results. The Points per serving would be 4½.

MINCED MEAT KEBABS
Kefta Kebab

POINTS

per recipe: 17½   per serving: 4½

Serves 4
Preparation and cooking time:
30 minutes + 1 hour chilling
Calories per serving: 210
Freezing: not recommended

On the streets of Morocco, Tunisia and Algeria, these fragrant kebabs are served in warmed pitta breads with a sprinkling of salt and cumin. They are delicious with Yogurt and Cucumber Dip (page 13) and Hummous (page 13); just remember to add the extra Points.

400 g (14 oz) lean minced lamb
a small bunch of parsley, chopped
a small bunch of coriander, chopped
1 onion, chopped finely
½ teaspoon ground allspice
¼ teaspoon cayenne pepper
1 teaspoon ground cumin
1 teaspoon paprika
low-fat cooking spray
salt and freshly ground black pepper
4 medium pitta breads, to serve

1 Mix all the ingredients except the low-fat cooking spray to a smooth paste in a bowl.
2 With moistened hands, take generous tablespoons of the paste and mould it into 10 cm (4-inch) long finger shapes around 4 wooden or metal skewers. Refrigerate for 1 hour.
3 Preheat the grill and cover a grill pan with foil. Spray with the cooking spray, then put the skewers on it and grill for 4 minutes on each side. To serve, slide off the skewers into pittas.

COOK'S TIPS If the mince falls off the skewers in step 2, put it in the fridge for 30 minutes and try again.

If using wooden skewers, soak them in water for 10 minutes before using so that they will not burn under the grill.

FRENCH LAMB CASSEROLE
Cassoulet

POINTS

per recipe: 25½   **per serving: 6½**

Serves 4
Preparation time: 10 minutes
Cooking time: 2½ hours
Calories per serving: 285
Freezing: recommended

This French dish cooks conveniently slowly in the oven while you go and do something else.

---

400 g (14 oz) dried haricot beans, soaked overnight or 2 × 300 g cans of haricot beans, drained

---

low-fat cooking spray

2 onions, chopped

3 garlic cloves, crushed

250 g (9 oz) lean cubed lamb

2 tablespoons tomato purée

400 g can of chopped tomatoes

2 sprigs of thyme

2 sprigs of majoram

2 sprigs of parsley

1 celery stalk, chopped roughly

1 bay leaf

a handful of chopped fresh parsley, to garnish

salt and freshly ground black pepper

---

1 If using the dried beans, drain the soaked beans and put in a saucepan. Cover with cold water. Bring to the boil and boil for 10 minutes, skimming occasionally. If using the canned beans, go directly to step 2.

2 Preheat the oven to Gas Mark 4/ 180°C/350°F. Spray a flameproof casserole with the cooking spray, then sauté the onions and garlic for 4 minutes on the hob. Add a couple of tablespoons of water if they stick. Add the meat and seal all over for 2 minutes.

3 Add the rest of the ingredients and 450 ml (16 fl oz) of water. Cover and bake for 2 hours, stirring every now and then. Add the seasoning and serve sprinkled with some fresh parsley.

Spanish Meatballs: One of Spain's favourite tapas dishes.

SPANISH MEATBALLS
Albondigas

POINTS

per recipe: 22½   **per serving: 5½**

Serves 4
Preparation time: 20 minutes
Cooking time: 45 minutes
Calories per serving: 295
Freezing: recommended

Albondigas are found everywhere in Spain.

---

400 g (14 oz) minced lamb

1 onion, grated coarsely

3 garlic cloves, crushed

1 egg

30 g (1¼ oz) ground almonds

1 teaspoon paprika

1 tablespoon ground cumin

¼ teaspoon ground cinnamon

a small bunch of parsley, chopped finely

salt and freshly ground black pepper

FOR THE SAUCE

1 tablespoon fennel seeds

150 ml (¼ pint) apple juice

400 g can of chopped tomatoes

1 tablespoon tomato purée

---

1 Put all the meatball ingredients into a bowl and mix thoroughly. With moistened hands, take small handfuls of the mixture and roll into 20 walnut-sized balls.

2 Make the sauce by dry-frying the fennel seeds for 2 minutes, then add the apple juice and boil for 2 more minutes. Then add the tomatoes and tomato purée diluted in 150 ml (¼ pint) water. Season. Simmer gently for 10 minutes.

3 Add the meatballs and make sure they are all covered by the sauce. Cover and simmer for 20–30 minutes. Turn them carefully once or twice during the cooking and add more water if needed.

French Lamb
Casserole:
A filling lamb
and bean
dish from the
Languedoc
region in
France.

Chocolate Roulade: A dream dessert for chocolate lovers.

desserts

In the Mediterranean, a meal is not complete until the fresh fruit has been served – yet another healthy food habit we would all do well to adopt. These recipes are simple to make and have been adapted to help you lose weight without compromising any of the fresh and vibrant flavours!

CHOCOLATE ROULADE

POINTS	
per recipe: 23½	per serving: 3

Ⓥ *Serves 8*

Preparation time: 20 minutes + cooling

Cooking time: 30 minutes

Calories per serving: 165

Freezing: not recommended

Here is a low-fat version of this delectable French dessert, ideal for any special occasion.

150 g (5½ oz) caster sugar
8 egg whites
a pinch of cream of tartar
50 g (1¾ oz) cocoa powder
1½ teaspoons vanilla extract

FOR THE FILLING

200 ml (7 fl oz) low-fat plain yogurt
50 g (1¾ oz) white cooking chocolate, melted
1 tablespoon caster sugar
1 teaspoon vanilla
200 g (7 oz) fresh raspberries, a few reserved for decoration
cocoa powder, for dusting
mint sprigs, to serve

1 Preheat the oven to Gas Mark 4/ 180°C/350°F. Grease a 33 × 23 cm (13 × 9-inch) Swiss roll tin. Lay a large sheet of greaseproof baking parchment on the work surface and dust it evenly with 2 tablespoons of the caster sugar.

2 Place the egg whites in a bowl with the cream of tartar and whisk until they form soft peaks.

3 Add the remaining caster sugar a little at a time and continue to whisk until thick and glossy. Fold in the cocoa and vanilla extract very carefully, taking care not to knock out the air.

4 Scrape the mixture into the prepared baking tin, taking it right into the corners. Bake for 30 minutes until firm and springy to the touch.

5 Leave the roulade to cool in the tin, then turn out on to the greaseproof baking parchment.

6 To make the filling, mix together the ingredients and then spread evenly over the unrolled roulade. Then roll up using the greaseproof baking parchment to help. Dust with cocoa powder and decorate with more fresh raspberries and mint sprigs to serve.

SICILIAN CASSATA

POINTS

| per recipe: 37½ | per serving: 3 |

V Serves 12
Preparation time: 10 minutes
Freezing time: 10 hours
Calories per serving: 215
Freezing: recommended

This frozen ricotta cake is very easy to make and can be made in advance.

8 trifle sponges or sponge fingers
6 tablespoons red fruit juice, e.g. forest fruits or raspberry
250 g (9 oz) ricotta cheese
100 g (3½ oz) icing sugar, sifted
250 ml (9 fl oz) low-fat plain yogurt
50 g (1¾ oz) shelled pistachios, chopped
50 g (1¾ oz) ready-to-eat tropical fruit mix, diced finely
100 g (3½ oz) fresh blueberries, washed
150 g (5½ oz) fresh strawberries, washed and chopped into small pieces
200 g (7 oz) 'no artificial colouring' glacé cherries, diced finely
a few fresh cherries, to garnish (optional)

1 Slice the trifle sponges in half through their centres so that they remain the same size but are thinner. Use to line the base of a 23 cm (9-inch) springform cake tin, trimming the sponges to fit the tin so that there are no gaps. Sprinkle the fruit juice over the sponges.

2 In a large bowl whip the ricotta with the icing sugar until smooth. Then add the yogurt, nuts and all the fruit except the fresh cherries.

3 Spoon into the cake tin on top of the sponges and freeze for at least 10 hours until firm and easy to slice.

4 To serve, unmould on to a plate and garnish with fresh cherries if using.

Lemon Polenta Cake: Ideal for afternoon tea or the perfect way to finish a Mediterranean meal.

LEMON POLENTA CAKE

POINTS

| per recipe: 27½ | per serving: 2½ |

V Serves 12
Preparation time: 15 minutes
Cooking time: 30 minutes
Calories per serving: 150
Freezing: not recommended

Polenta is an Italian cornmeal that colours this cake a pretty yellow and gives it a subtle crunch. It is now available in quick-cook varieties in most supermarkets now. It makes the perfect accompaniment to strawberries and low-fat crème fraîche, adding the extra Points. This dessert can be served warm or cold, cut into slices.

low-fat cooking spray
115 g (4 oz) polenta (ordinary or quick-cook)
115 g (4 oz) plain flour
1½ teaspoons baking powder
2 large eggs, plus 3 egg whites
175 g (6 oz) caster sugar
grated zest and juice of 2 lemons
1 teaspoon vanilla extract
200 ml (7 fl oz) low-fat plain yogurt
icing sugar, for dusting

1 Preheat the oven to Gas Mark 4/ 180°C/350°F. Spray the base of a 25 cm (10-inch) spring-form cake tin with low-fat cooking spray. Dust the tin with a little polenta.

2 Sift the flour and baking powder together into a bowl, then stir in the polenta.

3 In a separate bowl, whisk the whole eggs, egg whites and sugar together until pale and thick.

4 Add the polenta mixture, lemon zest and juice, vanilla and yogurt. Carefully fold in using a large metal spoon.

5 Spoon the mixture into the prepared tin and bake for 30 minutes.

6 Turn out on to a cooling rack and dust with icing sugar.

Sicilian Cassata:
This dessert
looks stunning
and is suprisingly
low in fat.

Italian Trifle: Fruity,
refreshing and
satisfying.

ITALIAN TRIFLE

POINTS

per recipe: 28   per serving: 7

Ⓥ *Serves 4*

Preparation time: 5 minutes
Chilling time: 30 minutes
Calories per serving: 270
Freezing: not recommended

This velvety smooth Italian dessert is absolutely delicious.

4 trifle sponges
250 g (9 oz) ricotta cheese
100 g (3½ oz) low-fat soft cheese
2 tablespoons reduced sugar jam with extra fruit
450 g (1 lb) fresh or frozen mixed strawberries, raspberries and blueberries in total
400 g can of peach slices in juice
2 drops of vanilla essence

1 Line the bottom of a large glass trifle bowl or four individual bowls with the trifle sponges.

2 In a separate bowl, beat together the ricotta, low-fat soft cheese and jam.

3 Quarter the strawberries, if using fresh ones, and mix with the other berries, peach slices and juice and vanilla essence in a bowl. Spoon this mixture over the sponges.

4 Spread the cheese mixture evenly over the fruit and decorate with more berries and mint leaves. Refrigerate for at least 30 minutes before serving.

CARAMELISED ORANGES

POINTS

per recipe: 7½   per serving: 2

Ⓥ *Serves 4*

Preparation time: 10 minutes +
2 hours chilling
Cooking time: 15 minutes
Calories per serving: 160
Freezing: not recommended

This Spanish dessert is the perfect end to a rich meal. The caramel melts while the oranges chill!

4 oranges
100 g (3½ oz) caster sugar
1 tablespoon orange flower water (optional)

1 Peel and slice the oranges, reserving the juice, and arrange in a shallow serving dish.

2 Place the sugar in a saucepan with 300 ml (10 fl oz) water and heat gently without stirring. Swirl the pan occasionally until the sugar has dissolved. Bring to the boil and continue boiling until it turns a rich golden brown, approximately

5 minutes. Remove immediately from the heat and stir in the reserved orange juice from step 1 and the orange flower water. Be careful as it will bubble and spit.

3 Pour the caramel over the oranges and refrigerate for at least 2 hours before serving.

COMPOTE OF DRIED FRUIT

POINTS

per recipe: 23½   per serving: 6

Ⓥ *Serves 4*

Preparation time: 5 minutes +
30 minutes cooling
Cooking time: 15 minutes
Calories per serving: 355
Freezing: not recommended

This French recipe makes a tasty and nutritious dessert. It's also delicious for breakfast with low-fat plain yogurt; just add the extra Points.

115 g (4 oz) dried apricots
250 g can of prunes in juice
115 g (4 oz) dried peaches or pears, halved
115 g (4 oz) dried figs, halved
60 g (2 oz) sultanas
100 g (3½ oz) sugar
2 tablespoons orange flower water or rose water (optional)

1 Wash all the fruit and then put it in a saucepan with 1 litre (1¾ pints) water and sugar. Bring to the boil, ' then cover and simmer for 15 minutes.

2 Leave to cool for at least 30 minutes, then add the orange flower water or rose water, if using. Transfer to a bowl and refrigerate until needed.

VARIATION Serve sprinkled with 2 tablespoons chopped pistachio nuts.